MW00475201

Stylish
Leather Jewelry

Modern Designs for Earrings, Bracelets, Necklaces, and More

Myléne Hillam

Design Originals

an Imprint of Fox Chapel Publishing
www.d-originals.com

Acquisition editor: Peg Couch
Copy editor: Ayleen Stellhorn
Cover and layout designer:
Ashley Millhouse
Cover and project photography:
Scott Kriner
Editor: Katie Weeber

ISBN 978-1-57421-401-7

© 2014 by Myléne Hillam and New Design Originals Corporation, www.d-originals.com, an imprint of Fox Chapel Publishing, 800-457-9112, 1970 Broad Street, East Petersburg, PA 17520.

Library of Congress Cataloging-in-Publication Data

Hillam, Myléne.
 Stylish leather jewelry / Myléne Hillam.
     pages cm
 Includes index.

  Summary: "Leather jewelry doesn't have to be traditional! Fabulous leather can be anything from casual and fun to stylish and sophisticated. With a smattering of beads and some clever construction ideas you can take leather jewelry beyond conventional and onto the fashion runway. Award-winning jewelry designer Myléne Hillam shows you how to use leather not just as a stringing component, but as the featured material in designer accessories. No conventional leather crafting skills are required. You'll learn how to loop, twist, fold, and recolor leather in ways that will redefine your perception of jewelry. Whether you're looking for something colorful and fun to team with your T-shirt and jeans or a statement necklace to dress up your work wear, you're bound to find something here to suit your style and take your wardrobe from glum to glam"-- Provided by publisher.

  ISBN 978-1-57421-401-7 (pbk.)
 1. Leatherwork. 2. Jewelry making. I. Title.
 TT290.H53 2014
 745.594'2--dc23
                   2013044746

Printed in the United States of America
First printing

Introduction

When I think of leather jewelry, western wear and Greek island and boho style are the first things that spring to mind. They're all traditional styles that have stood the test of time.

But leather jewelry doesn't have to be traditional. Combine leather with a smattering of beads, or use some clever construction ideas, and you can take your leather jewelry beyond conventional and onto the fashion runway. Think chic, think stylish, think upscale, and you'll arrive at designs like the ones in this book.

These designs are modern and fashion-forward and combine leather and beads in a way that will have you asking, "Is that really leather?" And the answer is a resounding, "Yes!"

Including leather in your designs will expand your jewelry-making skills and add a new dimension to your jewelry repertoire. Leather is not just a stringing material, but a material that can be manipulated to make beads, chains, and focal pieces. Don't let working with leather intimidate you—no traditional leather-crafting skills are required here. Instead, you'll learn how to loop, twist, fold, and recolor leather using simple techniques that I will teach you, step-by-step. And that's not all—I have many other ideas in store that you can use to add leather to your designs.

The techniques and ideas found here will redefine your perception of what leather jewelry is! So whether you're looking for something colorful and fun to pair with your T-shirt and jeans, or a statement necklace to dress up your work wear, you're bound to find something that suits your style within the pages of this book.

So let's get to work and start pushing boundaries!

Myléne

—Myléne Hillam

Contents

18 SUEDE LACE DESIGNS

32 BRAIDING AND WEAVING

Getting Started

Before you dive into jewelry making, it's a good idea to familiarize yourself with the basic tools, materials, and techniques you'll find throughout this book—especially if you're a beginner. This chapter will give you all the basic information you'll need to achieve success with the projects. Make sure you have the necessary tools on hand, stock up on all of the supplies you'll need, and practice some of the essential techniques so you have them down before you have to use them for a project.

Materials and Tools

Before you get underway with the designing of your leather jewelry, it's worth taking a look at all the types of leather and leather lacing used in this book. I've only listed the leather products I used in these projects, but there are many more available. Visit your local craft store to learn more.

Sof-Suede lace: Made from pigskin leather, Sof-Suede lace has a consistent color right through the lace. Its top is sueded, while its back is smooth. You should keep this in mind when making designs where both the front and the back of the lace will be seen. It's soft, flexible, very strong, and has little stretch. It's available in an extensive range of colors.

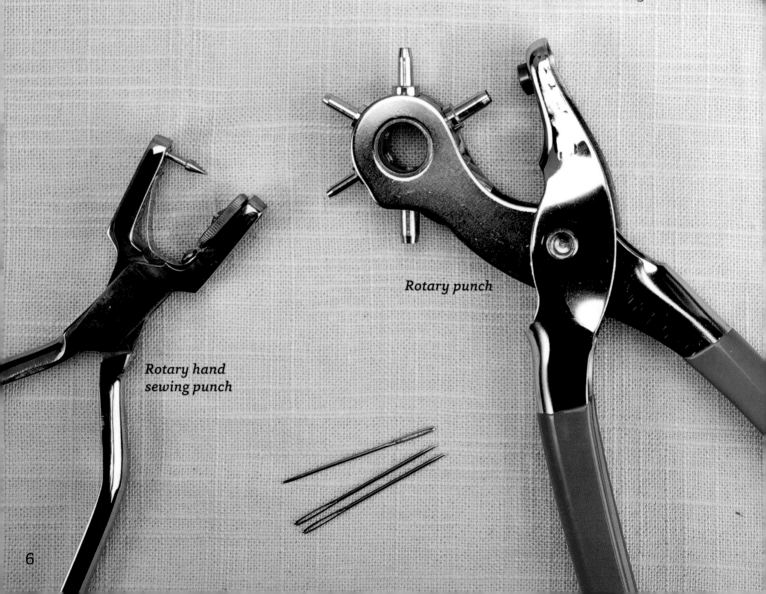

Rotary punch

Rotary hand sewing punch

Suede lace (A): This product is a heavier weight of suede than Sof-Suede lace, and it's made from cowhide splits. It consists of an inner layer and sueded outer layers, with the core color often being different than the suede color. This variation gives you the advantage of an extra color, when the lace is viewed from the side, without extra bulk. Suede lace has no obvious front or back, making it suitable for designs in which both sides will be visible. It comes in a variety of colors and widths.

Round leather cord (B): This versatile cord can be strung, woven, and knotted. Round leather cord is finished with a non-peel coating, so it will keep its good looks even after it has been added to a project. Leather cord is available in metallic finishes, as well as neutral colors, and also comes in a variety of diameters.

Deerskin lace (C): Smooth and soft to the touch, deerskin lace is a beautiful lace to wear against your skin. It's supple, lightweight, and very strong. It's a great choice for weaving and braiding because of its flexibility.

Leather trim and bracelet blanks: These project-sized pieces of leather are available in neutrals and metallics, as well as "hair on" animal prints, which are especially fun to work with! Some are firm, while others are soft and flexible, making them suitable for a wide variety of techniques. They can be cut to suit your project with scissors or a utility knife.

BASIC JEWELRY-MAKING TOOLS

In addition to the leather products listed, you'll need some jewelry-making tools to create the designs in this book.

From left to right: Memory wire shears, standard crimping pliers, flush cutters, and large crimping pliers (shown on page 9).

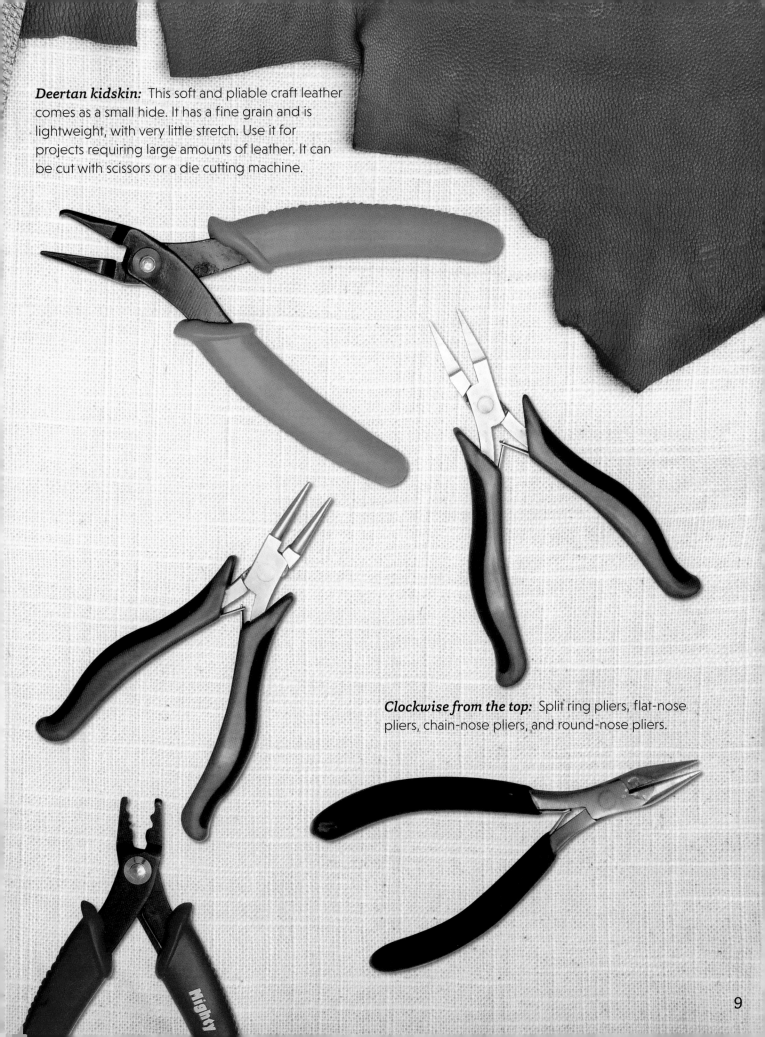

Deertan kidskin: This soft and pliable craft leather comes as a small hide. It has a fine grain and is lightweight, with very little stretch. Use it for projects requiring large amounts of leather. It can be cut with scissors or a die cutting machine.

Clockwise from the top: Split ring pliers, flat-nose pliers, chain-nose pliers, and round-nose pliers.

Basic Jewelry-Making Techniques

A basic knowledge of jewelry-making techniques is required to make the designs in this book. The following skills will help you assemble the jewelry. As with any new skill, practice makes perfect, so if you're new to jewelry making, practice before you tackle these techniques in conjunction with a project.

OPENING AND CLOSING A JUMP RING

1. Position the pliers. Thinking of the jump ring as a clock face, position it so the opening is at twelve o'clock. With a pair of chain-nose pliers in each hand, hold the jump ring between two o'clock and three o'clock in your right hand and between nine o'clock and ten o'clock in your left hand.

2. Open the jump ring. To open the jump ring, move one hand toward you, while moving the other hand away from you. Once open, a jump ring can be attached to any number of items, from findings to chain.

3. Check the shape. The jump ring should be opened from front to back, as if you are opening a door, not side to side, as if you are opening a book. Opening the jump ring from front to back allows it to keep its shape. To close the jump ring, repeat Step 2 in reverse.

OPENING AND CLOSING A SPLIT RING

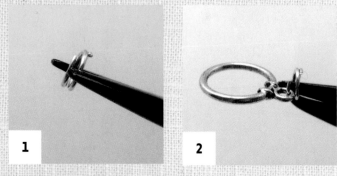

1. Open the split ring. Hold the split ring pliers in your dominant hand with the hooked jaw on top. Place the hook of the pliers in the channel of the split ring, between the two coils. Squeeze the handles of the pliers together to separate the coils of the ring and hold them open temporarily.

2. Attach the desired components. Hook the component you wish to attach onto the open end of the split ring. Remove the pliers from the coil and place the hooked jaw back in the coil a little further along. Slide the component along the coil. Repeat until the component reaches the end of the coil. Remove the pliers from the split ring to close it.

MAKING ROUND JUMP RINGS

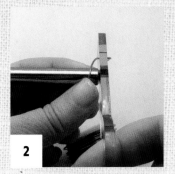

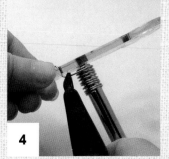

1. *Secure the end of the wire.* Thread one end of the wire, while it is still on the spool, through the hole of the turning handle of a jump ring mandrel. Secure it by folding it over.

2. *Begin to shape the wire.* Wrap the wire around the top of the mandrel and hold it in place with the thumb of your nondominant hand.

3. *Create a coil.* Place the index finger of your dominant hand in the hole of the turning handle and rotate it to create a coil around the mandrel.

4. *Trim.* Cut any excess wire from both ends of the coil.

5. *Cut the jump rings.* Slide the coil off the mandrel and cut each individual jump ring away from the coil.

> ### Tip
> For oval jump rings, snip each one while the coil is on the mandrel. Oval jump rings should be snipped halfway along the long side.

MAKING TRIANGULAR JUMP RINGS

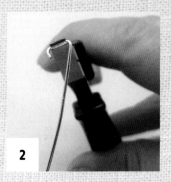

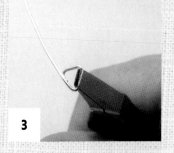

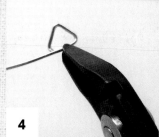

1. *Place the wire tip.* Place the tip of the wire so it sits halfway across the jaws of the flat-nose pliers. Bend the wire at a 60° angle to form the left prong and first corner of the triangle.

2. *Form the second corner.* Place the jaws of the pliers on the other side of the bend and make another 60° bend. This is the second corner of the triangle.

3. *Form the third corner.* Place the jaws of the pliers on the other side of the bend made in Step 2 and make a 60° bend. This creates the right prong and third corner of the triangle.

4. *Trim the wire.* Trim the end of the wire so the two prongs on either side of the opening are the same size.

5. *Check the shape.* Your completed triangle jump ring should look like this.

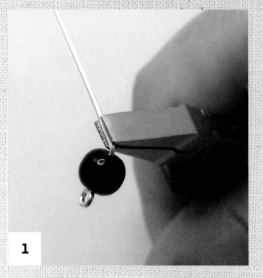

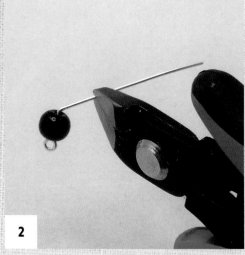

1. Bend the wire. Using the flat-nose pliers, bend the wire tail of the eye pin at a 45°–90° angle.

2. Trim the wire. Trim the tail of the eye pin to approximately ⅜" (1cm).

3. Shape the loop. Place the tip of the eye pin tail in the jaws of the round-nose pliers so you can just see the end of it. Rotate your wrist toward you as far as it will comfortably turn.

4. Reposition the pliers. Open the pliers. Rotate your wrist away from you so your palm is facing up, and regrip the wire at the same position along the pliers as before.

5. Finish the loop. Rotate your wrist toward you again until the loop is completed.

6. Check the shape. The completed simple loop should look like this.

MAKING A WRAPPED LOOP

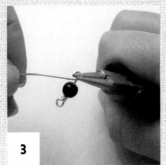

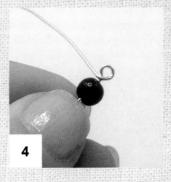

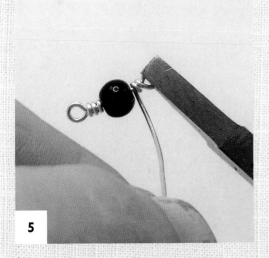

1. *Bend the wire.* You need approximately 1½" (4cm) of wire above the bead. Grip the wire above the bead with the tip of the chain-nose pliers. Bend the wire above the jaws of the pliers at a 45°–90° angle, creating a stem.

2. *Position the pliers.* Place the bottom jaw of the round-nose pliers in the bend.

3. *Form a loop.* Wrap the wire around the jaws of the pliers to create a loop, making sure the loop is centered above the stem.

4. *Cross the wire.* Cross the tail of the wire over the bend in the stem.

5. *Wrap the wire.* Grip the loop with the flat-nose pliers. Hold the tail of the wire and wrap the wire around the stem two or three times.

6. *Trim.* Trim away the excess with the flush cutters.

7. *Check the shape.* The completed wrapped loop should look like this.

CRIMPING BASICS

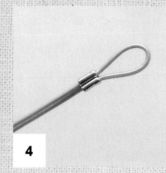

1. *String the crimp tube.* Double over a strand of beading wire to form a loop in the center. String a crimp tube onto both ends of the wire and bring it up to the loop.

2. *Make the first crimp.* Place the crimp tube in the second hole of the crimping pliers (the one closest to the handles). Make sure the two strands of beading wire do not cross over each other, and the wire loop is parallel to the pliers. Then, gently squeeze the crimp tube.

3. *Make the second crimp.* Place the crimp tube in the first hole of the crimping pliers (farthest from the handles), positioning it so the beading wire loop is perpendicular to the side of the pliers. Squeeze the crimp so the two channels are compressed. Tug the wires to make sure they are secure.

4. *Check the shape.* Once crimped, the tube should look like this.

MAKING A MEMORY WIRE LOOP

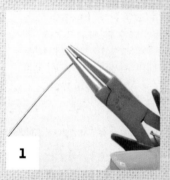

Tip

For an outward-facing loop (shown), form the loop on the outside curve of the wire. For an inward facing loop, form the loop on the inside curve.

1. *Begin the loop.* Grip the tip of the memory wire with the round-nose pliers and rotate your wrist toward you.

2. *Reposition the pliers.* Release the wire, rotate your wrist away from you so your palm is facing up, and regrip the wire. Turn your wrist toward you as far as it will comfortably turn.

3. *Finish the loop.* With the partly formed loop still on the pliers, use your other hand to wrap the tail end of the wire around the jaw to meet the loop end. This will give you a fully rounded loop.

ATTACHING RIBBON CLAMPS

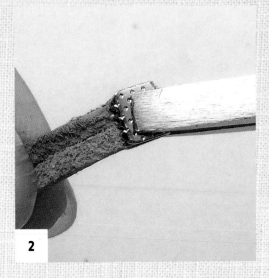

Tip
If desired, add a drop of glue to the ends of the leather before attaching the ribbon clamps for extra security.

1. Position the leather. Align the ends of the leather strands.

2. Position the clamp. Place the ribbon clamp over the ends of the leather pieces so the leather ends are flush with the top of the ribbon clamp. Using flat-nose pliers, gently, but firmly, squeeze the clamp onto the leather until it is secure.

ATTACHING END CAPS

1. Apply the epoxy to the leather. Mix an epoxy adhesive (I use 5 Minute Epoxy) according to the manufacturer's instructions and apply it to the end of the leather. Apply enough so the end cap will be secure, but not so much that it will ooze out from under the end cap.

2. Apply the epoxy to the end cap. Also apply epoxy to the inside of the end cap with a toothpick.

3. Attach the end cap. Push the leather into the end cap.

4. Touch up as needed. Remove any excess epoxy with acetone if needed.

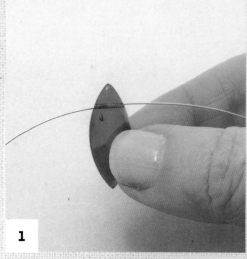

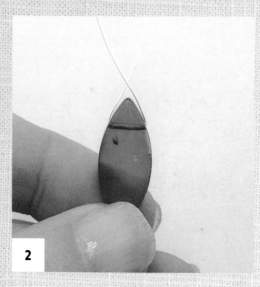

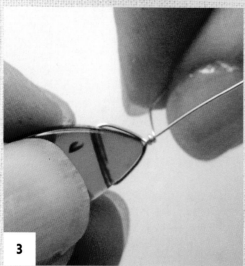

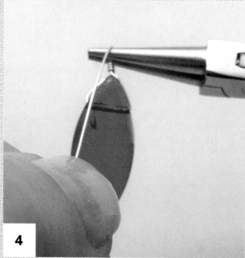

1. *Thread the bead.* Thread the end of a piece of wire through the bead, leaving a 1" (2.5cm) tail.

2. *Bend the wire.* Bend the wire at the point where it exits the holes in the bead. Bring the wire ends to the center point above the bead.

3. *Wrap the wire.* Bend the long wire vertically so it extends from the top of the bead. Wrap the short wire three times around the stem of the long wire and then trim away the excess.

4. *Form a loop.* Grip the long wire above the wraps with the round-nose pliers and wrap the wire around the jaws of the pliers, creating a loop. The direction the loop faces will depend on your design. In this example, the loop is perpendicular to the bead face.

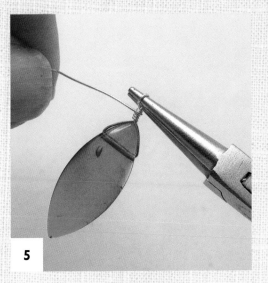

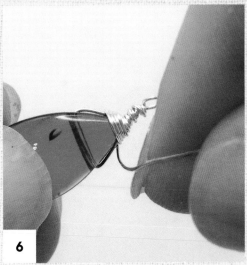

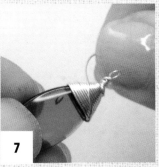

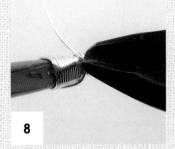

5. *Wrap the wire.* Wrap the long wire around the stem over the three existing loops.

6. *Begin wrapping the bead.* Keep wrapping the wire down over the top of the bead.

7. *Finish wrapping the bead.* Continue wrapping the bead until you have reached the bead holes. Take the wire back up to the stem and wrap it two or three times to secure it.

8. *Trim.* Trim away the excess wire.

9. *Check your progress.* The completed wrapped top-drilled bead should look like this.

Tip

This technique is most easily done with fine-gauge wire, such as 26-gauge. I like to use a non-tarnishing wire so the wire always stays bright and shiny.

Suede Lace Designs

If you love color, then you'll love creating jewelry with suede lace. With a palette ranging from pastels and brights to earth tones and neutrals, you can choose a color scheme that conveys the mood of your design, such as the earthy tribal tones of the Zulu Princess Choker (page 26), the beach-inspired Sand and Surf Neck Tickler Earrings (page 20), or the luxurious rainforest shades of the Peacock Earrings (page 24). Or you can simply choose a palette that will suit your outfit. Either way, suede lace gives you so many color options!

In this section, you'll discover how soft and flexible suede lace is and how it can be used to build designs using repetitive patterns. Whether it's looped, scrolled, or segmented, suede lace jewelry can be anything—from casual and fun to stylish and sophisticated.

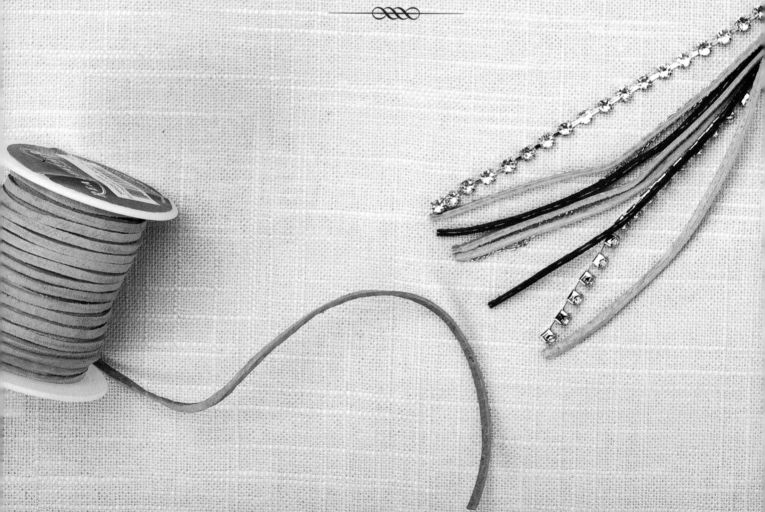

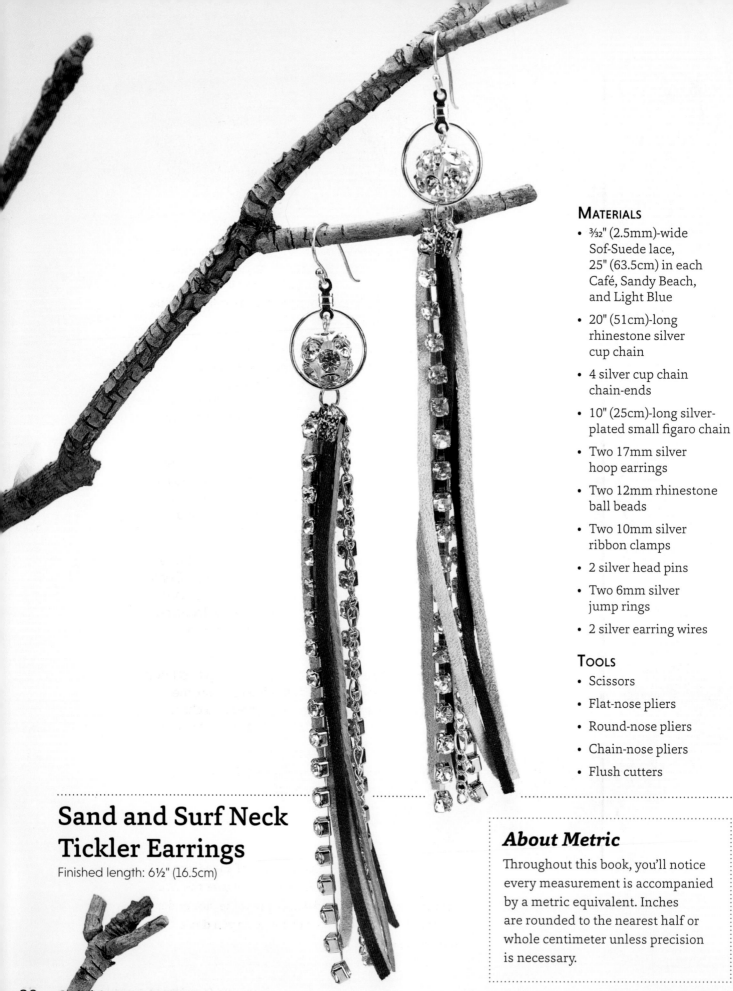

MATERIALS

- ³⁄₃₂" (2.5mm)-wide Sof-Suede lace, 25" (63.5cm) in each Café, Sandy Beach, and Light Blue
- 20" (51cm)-long rhinestone silver cup chain
- 4 silver cup chain chain-ends
- 10" (25cm)-long silver-plated small figaro chain
- Two 17mm silver hoop earrings
- Two 12mm rhinestone ball beads
- Two 10mm silver ribbon clamps
- 2 silver head pins
- Two 6mm silver jump rings
- 2 silver earring wires

TOOLS

- Scissors
- Flat-nose pliers
- Round-nose pliers
- Chain-nose pliers
- Flush cutters

Sand and Surf Neck Tickler Earrings

Finished length: 6½" (16.5cm)

About Metric

Throughout this book, you'll notice every measurement is accompanied by a metric equivalent. Inches are rounded to the nearest half or whole centimeter unless precision is necessary.

1

2

3

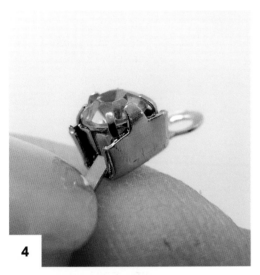

4

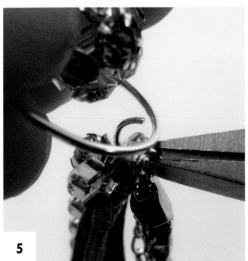

5

1. *Attach the rhinestone.* String a rhinestone ball bead onto a head pin and turn a simple loop (see page 12). Attach the simple loop to the inside loop of an earring hoop. Attach an earring wire to the outside loop of the earring hoop.

2. *Cut and align the suede lace.* Cut two 5" (12.5cm) lengths of each of the three colors of suede lace for six pieces total. Cut two 5" (12.5cm) lengths of the rhinestone cup chain and one 5" (12.5cm) length of the figaro chain. Align the cut ends of three different lace colors.

3. *Secure the suede lace.* Place the remaining three laces on top of the first three, making sure that no two pieces of the same color are on top of each other. Place the ends of the laces in a ribbon clamp and gently squeeze until all the laces are secure.

4. *Attach the chain-ends.* Place the first rhinestone cup of the rhinestone cup chain in a chain-end. Gently squeeze the chain-end prongs with chain-nose pliers to hold the rhinestone cup in place. Repeat to attach a chain-end to one end of the second length of rhinestone cup chain.

5. *Complete the earring.* Open a jump ring and hook on one rhinestone cup chain, the figaro chain, the ribbon clamp with lace, and the second cup chain. Before closing the jump ring, attach it to the bottom loop of the earring hoop.

6. *Make the second earring.* Repeat Steps 1–5 to make a second matching earring.

Tip

To straighten out the kinks and coils of suede lace, use an iron and a towel. Place the towel over the lace, set the iron to steam, and gently press the lace under the towel. Use short bursts of steam so you don't scorch the suede.

MATERIALS

- ⅛" (3mm)-wide suede lace, 35" (89cm) in Turquoise
- Two 12mm blue/yellow hollow glass beads
- Eight 4mm amber glass bicones
- Four 6mm light blue glass rounds
- Two 61mm silver head pins
- Two 30mm silver eye pins
- 2 silver earring wires

TOOLS

- Scissors
- Flat-nose pliers
- Chain-nose pliers
- Round-nose pliers
- Flush cutters
- Rotary hand sewing punch
- Ruler
- Permanent marker

Scroll Earrings
Finished length: 3⅜" (8.5cm)

1

2

3

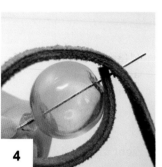

4

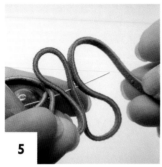

5

6

1. *Measure and mark the lace.* Cut a 15¼"
(38.5cm) length of lace for each earring. Measure and
place a mark at the following positions on each lace
piece: 2" (5cm), 3¾" (9.5cm), 6¼" (16cm), 8¾" (22cm),
10⅝" (27cm), and 12⁷⁄₁₆" (31.5cm). Place a mark
³⁄₃₂" (2.5mm) in from each end of the lace pieces.

2. *Punch the holes.* Set the hole punch to the smallest
setting and punch a hole at each mark, making sure
the holes are centered on the lace. Punch holes in
both pieces of lace.

3. *Begin stringing the earring.* On the head pin,
string on an amber bead and a hollow glass bead.
Thread on a piece of lace, beginning with the hole
³⁄₃₂" (2.5mm) from the end.

4. *Make the loop.* Wrap the lace around the hollow
glass bead, forming a loop, and thread the next hole
onto the head pin.

5. *Finish threading the lace.* Continue threading
the lace onto the head pin at each hole, weaving it
backward and forward to form a scroll design until
all the lace has been threaded. String on a blue glass
bead and an amber bicone. Turn a simple loop (see
page 12) at the end of the head pin.

6. *Complete the earring.* On the eye pin, string an
amber bicone, a blue round, and an amber bicone.
Turn a simple loop (see page 12) at the end. Connect
the simple loop of the eye pin to the simple loop of
the head pin. Open the loop of an earring wire and
hook on the connected beaded components.

7. *Make the second earring.* Repeat Steps 3–6 to
make a second matching earring.

MATERIALS

- ³⁄₃₂" (2.5mm)-wide Sof-Suede lace, 10" (25.5cm) in each Kiwi and Pacific Green
- ⅛" (3mm)-wide suede lace, 10" (25.5cm) in Turquoise
- Forty 4mm iris sapphire bicones
- 2 silver earring wires
- 5" (12.5cm), 20-gauge non-tarnish silver beading wire
- 15" (38cm), 24-gauge non-tarnish silver beading wire

TOOLS

- Chain-nose pliers
- Round-nose pliers
- Flat-nose pliers
- Flush cutters
- Rotary hand sewing punch
- Scissors
- Ruler
- Permanent marker

Peacock Earrings
Finished length: 2½" (6.5cm)

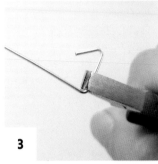
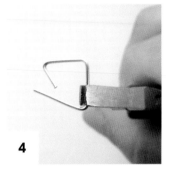

1. Punch the holes. Cut a 2¼" (5.5cm) length of Kiwi lace, a 2¾" (7cm) length of Turquoise lace, and a 3¼" (8.5cm) length of Pacific Green lace. Place a mark ⅛" (3mm) from each end of the laces. Set the hole punch to the smallest setting and punch a hole at each mark.

2. Begin the triangle jump ring. Create a triangle jump ring (see page 11) using the flat-nose pliers and 20-gauge wire. Start by creating the left prong at the base of the triangle. Hold the end of the wire flush with the jaws of the pliers. Bend the wire at a 45° angle. This will be the left side of the triangle.

3. Make the top bend. Take the wire out of the pliers and reposition the pliers so they are twice the width of the jaws from the first bend. Bend the wire at a 90° angle. You have now formed the top of the triangle.

4. Make the right side. Reposition the wire in the jaws again, making sure the jaws are twice their width from the top bend. Bend the wire again to create the right side of the triangle.

5. Finish the triangle jump ring. Complete the third bend by placing the jaws in the angle of the bend and trimming the wire to the width of the jaws to create the right prong at the base of the triangle.

6. String the wire. Cut a 4½" (11.5cm) length of 24-gauge wire. Create a simple loop (see page 12) on one end of the wire and string on twenty bicones. Making sure there are no gaps between the beads, trim the wire, leaving enough length to turn another simple loop (see page 12) at the other end.

7. Begin attaching the components. Open the triangle jump ring and thread one end of the beaded wire onto one of the prongs. Thread one end of each of the three laces onto the jump ring, starting with the longest.

8. Finish attaching the components. Repeat Step 7 on the other prong of the jump ring, threading on the other ends of the pieces already attached to form loops. Then, carefully bring the two prong ends back to the middle of the jump ring. Adjust the beaded and lace loops so they create a teardrop shape.

9. Complete the earring. Open the loop of an earring wire and thread on the triangle jump ring.

10. Make the second earring. Repeat Steps 1–9 to make a second matching earring.

MATERIALS

- ³⁄₃₂" (2.5mm)-wide Sof-Suede lace, 25" (63.5cm) in each Light Blue, Tiger Lily, Café, and Gold Nugget
- One hundred fourteen 3mm gold spacer beads
- One 30 x 25mm terracotta resin focal bead
- 3½" (9cm)-diameter gold necklace memory wire

TOOLS

- Memory wire shears
- Ruler
- Round-nose pliers
- Rotary hand sewing punch

Zulu Princess Choker

Finished length: 16½" (41cm)

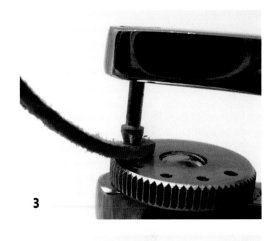

3

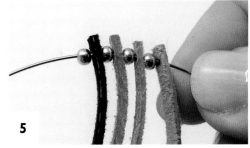

5

1. Cut the memory wire. Cut one and a half coils of memory wire and turn an outward-facing loop on one end (see page 14).

2. Cut the lace. Cut eight 2" (5cm) lengths of each color of Sof-Suede Lace for thirty-two pieces total. Cut one of each of the following lengths from the colors indicated: Café, 2⁷⁄₁₆" (6cm); Tiger Lily, 3⅞" (10cm); Gold Nugget, 5" (12.5cm); and Light Blue, 6⅜" (16cm).

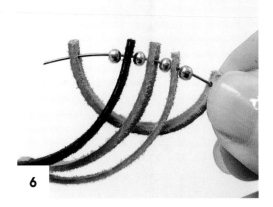

6

3. Punch the holes. Set the hole punch to the smallest setting and punch a hole ⅛" (3mm) from each end of every lace piece. Set the longer lengths aside to add to the middle of the choker later.

4. Begin stringing the beads. String twenty gold beads onto the memory wire.

5. Begin stringing the laces. Thread one end of a Light Blue lace onto the wire, followed by a gold bead. Continue threading, adding a Gold Nugget lace, a gold bead, a Tiger Lily lace, a gold bead, a Café lace, and a final gold bead.

6. Create the first loop. Thread the tail end of the Light Blue lace onto the wire, forming a loop. Make sure the lace loop passes behind the other laces.

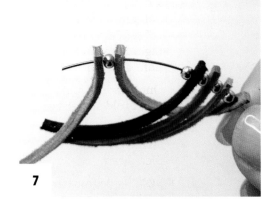

7

7. Add the next lace piece. String a gold bead onto the wire and another Light Blue lace.

8. Create the second loop. String a gold bead onto the wire and then thread on the tail end of the Gold Nugget lace, forming a loop. Make sure the Gold Nugget loop passes in front of the Light Blue loop already created, but behind the other laces.

9. Add the next lace piece. Add a gold bead and another Gold Nugget lace, followed by a gold bead.

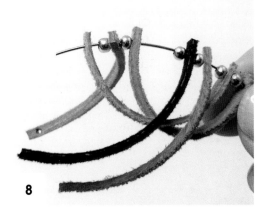

8

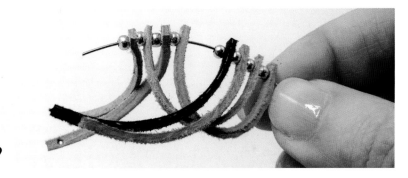

9

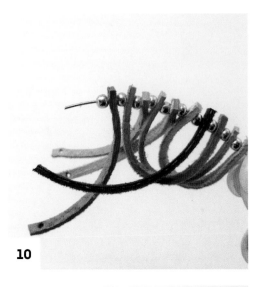

10

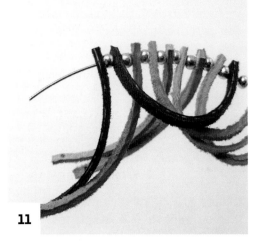

11

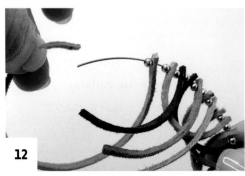

12

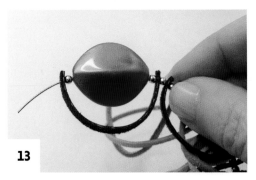

13

10. *Create the third loop and add the next piece.* Thread the [tail] end of the Tiger Lily lace onto the wire, forming a loop. Make sure it passes in front of the Light Blue and Gold Nugget loops, but behind the Café piece. Add a gold bead. Then, add another Tiger Lily lace and a gold bead.

11. *Create the fourth loop and add the next piece.* Thread the [tail] end of the Café lace onto the wire, forming a loop. Make sure it passes in front of all the other loops created previously, and add a gold bead. Add another Café lace and gold bead. This completes the first set of loops. Continue in this fashion (repeating Steps) until you have added four short laces of each color.

12. *Begin stringing the long laces.* After threading on the [tail] of the fourth short Light Blue lace, add one end of the long [Light] Blue lace set aside previously, followed by a gold bead. Continue the color pattern, threading the tail end of the next short lace, a [gold] bead, the corresponding long lace, and a gold bead.

13. *Add the focal bead.* After threading one end of the long Café lace and a gold bead, string on the focal bead, a gold bead, the tail of the long Café lace, and another gold bead. Add a short Café lace and gold bead.

14. *Finish stringing the long laces.* Thread the tail end of the long Tiger Lily lace onto the wire, making sure it passes behind the Café laces. Add a gold bead, a short Tiger Lily lace, and a gold bead. Thread the tail end of the long Gold Nugget lace onto the wire, making sure it passes behind the Tiger Lily and Café laces. Add a gold bead. Add a short Gold Nugget lace and gold bead. Thread the tail end of the long Light Blue lace onto the wire, making sure it passes behind the Gold Nugget, Tiger Lily, and Café laces. Add a gold bead. Add a short Light Blue lace and gold bead.

15. *Create the loops for the other side of the necklace.* Thread the tail end of the short Café lace added in Step 13 and a gold bead onto the wire. Make sure the lace passes in front of the long, center laces. Add a short Café lace and a gold bead.

16. *Finish the loops.* Continue the pattern of loops for the other side of the necklace, adding laces and gold beads until you have used up all the remaining short laces. Make sure the laces pass in front of the long center laces, but behind the loop just created.

17. *Complete the necklace.* String twenty gold beads onto the wire. Trim the end of the wire to ⅜" (1cm) and turn an outward-facing loop (see page 14).

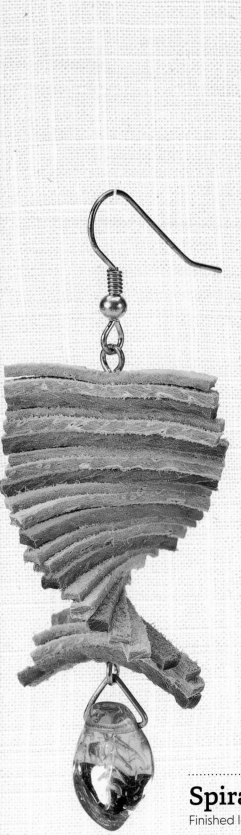

MATERIALS

- ³⁄₃₂" (2.5mm)-wide Sof-Suede lace, 20" (51cm) in each Tiger Lily, Pink, and Gold Nugget
- 2 copper-backed Czech glass leaf beads
- 4 copper eye pins
- 2 copper earring wires

TOOLS

- Scissors
- Chain-nose pliers
- Round-nose pliers
- Flat-nose pliers
- Flush cutters
- Permanent marker
- Ruler
- Rotary hand sewing punch

Spiral Wave Earrings

Finished length: 2⅞" (7.5cm)

2

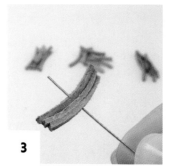

3

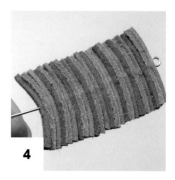

4

Tip

Use an eye pin instead of jewelry wire to create the triangle jump ring so all of the copper findings are the same color.

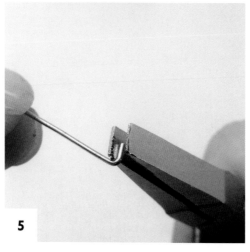

5

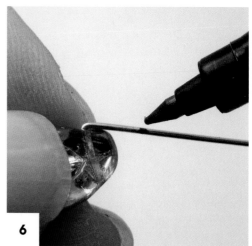

6

1. *Cut the lace pieces.* Cut eight 1" (25mm) lengths of each of the three colors of Sof-Suede lace for each earring (twenty-four pieces total for each earring).

2. *Punch the holes.* Mark the center of each lace piece with the permanent marker. Set the hole punch to the smallest setting and carefully line up the point of the punch with the mark. Punch a hole in each lace piece at the center mark.

3. *Begin threading the laces.* Thread the laces onto an eye pin in this order: Gold Nugget, Pink, and Tiger Lily. Repeat until eight of each color (twenty-four total) have been threaded on.

4. *Make a simple loop.* Push the laces firmly together and then make a simple loop (see page 12) at the end of the eye pin, facing in the opposite direction of the top loop (not shown in photo).

5. *Begin making a triangle jump ring.* Create a triangle jump ring (see page 11) from an eye pin. Place the end of the eye pin so it sits in the middle of the jaws of the flat-nose pliers. Bend a 60° angle to form the left prong at the base of the triangle.

6. *Mark the top bend.* Place the left prong of the triangle into a leaf bead and mark the place along the wire where the wire is directly above the point of the leaf bead.

7. *Make the top bend.* Remove the eye pin from the leaf bead and bend the wire at the mark made in Step 6 at a 60° angle.

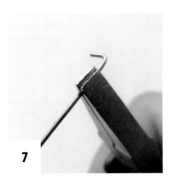

7

8

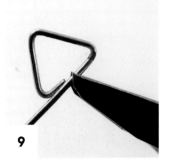

9

10

12

8. *Mark the right bend.* Place the left prong of the triangle back into the leaf bead, and mark the wire directly opposite the bead hole, where you will need to make the third bend to complete the triangle.

9. *Complete the triangle jump ring.* Remove the triangle jump ring from the bead and make the right bend at a 60° angle where marked. Trim the right prong of the triangle to match the left prong, cutting away the eye pin loop.

10. *Attach the triangle jump ring.* Carefully open the prongs of the triangle jump ring outward and insert the prongs into the holes on each side of the leaf bead. Push both prongs firmly into the bead.

11. *Attach the leaf bead.* Open the simple loop at the bottom of the eye pin with the laces and attach the leaf bead with the triangle jump ring.

12. *Complete the earring.* Open the top loop of the eye pin and attach an earring wire. Fan out the laces so they twist around the eye pin.

13. *Make the second earring.* Repeat Steps 3–12 to make a second matching earring.

Braiding and Weaving

In exploring all the different kinds of jewelry that can be made with leather, I just couldn't skip over the most traditional methods: braiding and weaving. With a bit of patience and rhythm, you can whip up a leather braid in no time at all. But while braiding and weaving might be seen as traditional, it doesn't mean your finished braided jewelry has to *look* traditional.

In this section, we will take a look at these traditional techniques, shake them up, add unexpected twists, throw in some creative jewelry construction ideas, and transform them from ordinary ideas into *extraordinary* jewelry. These techniques will change the way you look at braiding forever!

MATERIALS

- ³⁄₃₂" (2.5mm)-wide Sof-Suede lace, 20" (51cm) in Café and 15" (38cm) in Aqua

- 14" (35.5cm)-long, 15 x 20mm silver textured oval cable chain

- Two 10mm silver ribbon clamps

- 2 silver two-loop end connectors

- One 29 x 32mm round patinaed brass slider

- Four 6mm silver jump rings

- Eight 4mm silver jump rings

- 1 silver hitch and ball clasp

TOOLS

- Scissors
- Flat-nose pliers
- Chain-nose pliers
- Binder clip

Mint Chocolate Braided Chain Choker
Finished length: 16½" (42cm)

2

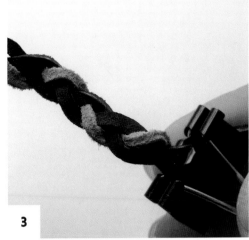

3

4

7

8

9

1. Cut the lace pieces. Cut two 9" (23cm) lengths of Café lace and one 9" (23cm) length of Aqua lace.

2. Clamp the lace ends. Line up the ends of the three lace pieces, placing the Aqua lace in the center. Place the ends in a ribbon clamp and clamp them securely with the flat-nose pliers.

3. Braid the laces. Braid the three lace pieces together, and then temporarily secure the loose ends with the binder clip.

4. Weave the braid. Measure 7" (18cm) along the chain and open the center link. Separate the chain into two equal pieces and close the link again. Weave the braided suede lace through the links of one chain length.

5. Attach the clasp. Open a 6mm jump ring and hook on one half of the hitch and ball clasp, the loop of the ribbon clamp, and the end link of the woven chain. Close the jump ring. Connect the other half of the clasp to the end link of the second chain length with a 6mm jump ring.

6. Secure the braid. Remove the binder clip from the braid and trim the loose ends of the suede lace pieces to the length of the chain. Place the ends in a ribbon clamp and securely clamp them in place.

7. Attach the jump rings. Connect the 4mm jump rings together in pairs so you have four sets of two jump rings each. Attach one set to each of the four loops on the back of the patinaed slider.

8. Attach the end connecters. Attach the other end of each set of jump rings to the outer holes of the end connectors.

9. Check your progress. Adding the end connectors will give your slider an extra special touch. It should look like this.

10. Attach the chain. Open a 6mm jump ring and use it to attach one end connector to the last link of the braided chain and the loop of the ribbon clamp. Repeat to connect the remaining chain length to the other end connector. Note: One side of the choker will have the suede braid woven into the chain. The other side will have chain without the suede braid.

MATERIALS

- ³⁄₁₆" (0.5cm)-wide deerskin lace, 20" (51cm) in Chocolate
- Two 13 x 19mm purple-and-blue flat oval glass beads with foil
- Two 4mm vintage rose crystal bicones
- Forty-six 6mm silver rope-patterned rings
- Two 6mm silver filigree bead caps
- Two 51mm silver ball head pins
- Two 4mm silver jump rings
- Four 6mm silver jump rings
- 2 silver earring wires

TOOLS

- Scissors
- Chain-nose pliers
- Round-nose pliers
- Rotary hand sewing punch
- Flush cutters
- Permanent marker
- Ruler

Jeweled Teardrop Earrings

Finished length: 2⁷⁄₈" (7.5cm)

1. String two rings. Cut 8" (20.5cm) of deerskin lace. String on two rings, positioning them 1" (2.5cm) from the end of the lace.

2. Bring the lace back. Thread the long end of the lace back through first ring.

3. Position the rings. Pull the ends of the lace so it is flat. Position the rings so the bottom of the second ring is secured underneath the lace and the ring is perpendicular to the lace.

4. Add the third ring. String another ring onto the long end of the lace and slide it up to the first two rings.

5. Bring the lace back. Bring the long end of the lace back through the second ring (the one positioned perpendicular to the lace) and pull it up.

6. Position the rings. The top of the third ring will be secured above the lace but will sit beneath the work. Position it perpendicular to the lace as you did with the second ring.

7. Add a fourth ring. String another ring onto the long end of the lace and slide it up to the other rings. Then, bring the long end of the lace back through the third ring (the one positioned perpendicular to the lace). Pull it up firmly.

8. Check the pattern. With four rings added, you can see the pattern emerge.

9

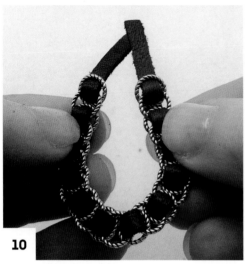

10

12

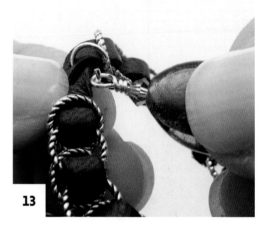

13

9. *Continue adding rings.* Continue adding rings in this fashion until you have a chain of twenty-three rings. Thread the lace through the last ring so it rests flat against the lace.

10. *Make a teardrop.* Bring the ends of the lace together to form a teardrop shape. Mark the center of the point where the two laces cross over each other at the top of the teardrop.

11. *Punch the holes.* Set the rotary punch to the smallest setting and punch a hole through each end of the lace at the marked locations. Trim away any excess lace on each end, and also trim off the point at the top that is formed when the laces cross.

12. *Create the center dangle.* String a bead cap, a flat oval bead, and a crystal bicone onto a head pin and create a wrapped loop (see page 13).

13. *Attach the center dangle.* Open a 6mm jump ring and thread it through the holes in the lace teardrop. Position the jump ring so the opening faces the bottom of the teardrop. Before closing it, add the center dangle.

14. *Add a jump ring.* Open a 4mm jump ring and thread it through the two holes in the lace teardrop. Position the jump ring so the opening faces away from the bottom of the teardrop and close it.

15. *Complete the earring.* Connect an earring wire to the jump ring you just added using another 4mm jump ring.

16. *Make the second earring.* Repeat Steps 1–15 to make a second matching earring.

MATERIALS

- 2mm round leather cord, 55" (140cm) in each Gold, Silver, Copper, and Metallic Brown
- 8" (20cm)-long, 6.1mm silver-plated oval link chain
- Six 8mm silver end caps
- Ten 7mm silver jump rings
- One 4mm silver jump ring
- Sewing thread
- Silver lobster claw clasp
- Epoxy adhesive (I used 5 Minute Epoxy)
- Toothpick

TOOLS

- Braiding disk
- Scissors
- Chain-nose pliers
- Flush cutters
- Binder clip

Soft Metal Fusion Kumihimo Necklace

Finished length: 21" (53.5cm)

2

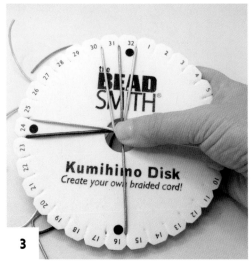

3

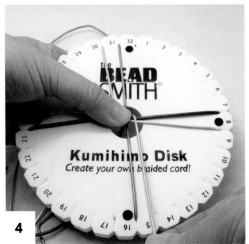

4

1. Cut the cord pieces. Cut a 20" length of each color of the four round leather cords.

2. Position the cords on the braiding disk. Find the center of the first cord and lay it across the hole in the braiding disk. Place one end of the cord into the slot to the left of the dot at the top of the disk. Pull the cord firmly and place the other end into the slot to the right of the bottom dot. Repeat with the second cord, placing the cord in the slot to the right of the top dot and the left of the bottom dot. Continue clockwise to place the remaining two cords on either side of the dots on each side of the disk, crossing them over the middle hole.

3. Complete the first braiding step. There are just three steps involved to braid the cords, and they are the same for both right handers and left handers. First, hold the center of the cords in place with your right thumb. With your left hand, lift the bottom left cord out of its slot and place it into the slot to the left of the cords at the top of the disk. You now have three cords at the top of the disk and one cord at the bottom.

4. Complete the second braiding step. Switch hands, placing your left thumb over the center of the cords. Using your right hand, lift the top right cord out of its slot and place it into the slot to the right of the cord at the bottom of the disk.

5. Complete the third braiding step. Rotate the disk counterclockwise. Repeat the three braiding steps until the cords are too short to reach their corresponding slots.

6. Secure the braid. Cut a 12" (30.5cm) length of sewing thread and tie the thread around the braid while it is still in the disk. Knot it securely and remove the braid from the disk without trimming the thread ends.

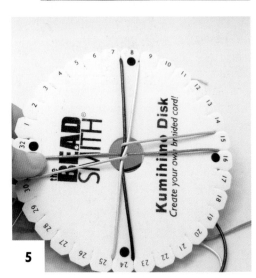

5

6

7

7. Wrap the braid. Secure the loose ends of the braid with the binder clip. Then, wrap the thread several times around the braid and tie it off in a knot. Set this braid aside.

8. Make a second braid. Repeating Steps 1–7, create a second Kumihimo braid. Tie it off with a length of sewing thread and remove it from the disk as before.

9. Mark the braid. Cut a length of thread and wrap it around one of the braids, 1½" (3cm) from the wrapped end. Leave a gap of ½" (1.5cm) and wrap another length of thread around the braid. Measure along 1½" (3cm) and wrap the braid again.

10. Cut the segments. Cut the braid between the ½" (1.5cm) gap. Then, trim away the excess leather cord. You should have two 1½" (3cm) braid segments.

11. Attach the end caps. Mix the epoxy adhesive according to the manufacturer's instructions and then apply it to the inside of an end cap with a toothpick. Firmly push one of the braid ends inside the end cap. Repeat, placing a cap on each end of all three braids.

12. Start the rings. Cut two 4½" (11cm) lengths of each Copper, Silver, and Gold cord for six pieces total. Create six leather rings by tying each piece into a circle measuring ⅝" (1.5cm) in diameter.

13. Finish the rings. Then, for each ring, weave both ends of the cord around the foundation circle until the ends meet.

14. Connect the rings. Form the rings into two chains by connecting them with 7mm jump rings. Make sure each chain contains one ring of each color and that the colors are in the same order.

15. Attach the braids. Shape the long braid into a curve. Use 7mm jump rings to attach each end of the long braid to the end of one of the ring chains. Attach each of the smaller braided pieces to the other end of the ring chains.

16. Attach the chain. Cut two 4" (10cm) lengths of chain and connect one to each end of the necklace. Attach the lobster claw to the end link of one of the chain lengths with a 4mm jump ring.

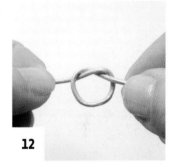

12

13

14

MATERIALS

- 2mm round leather cord, 100" (254cm) in Metallic Silver

- Two 15 x 15mm white/clear glass lentil beads

- 4 large-hole red glass and metal ring beads (I used Cousin Trinkettes® M34699-023)

- Four 5mm silver filigree bead caps

- Four 6mm silver jump rings

- 2 silver eye pins

- Two 12mm silver jump rings (if making your own, you will need a jump ring mandrel and 20-gauge non-tarnish silver wire)

- 1 silver fold-over magnetic clasp

- Leather adhesive

TOOLS

- Scissors
- Ruler
- Round-nose pliers
- Flat-nose pliers
- Chain-nose pliers
- Flush cutters

White Wreath Bracelet

Finished length: 6½" (16.5cm)

1

2

3

4

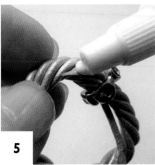
5

10

1. *Form a circle.* Cut a 30" (76cm) length of leather cord. String a glass and metal ring bead on one end and then form the cord into a 1⅜" (3.5cm) circle. Tie a half-knot in the cord so the ring bead is loose on the circle.

2. *Begin weaving the wreath.* Wrap the long end of the cord around the foundation circle four times, spacing the wraps evenly around the cord so you finish back at the half-knot.

3. *Continue weaving the wreath.* Slide the ring bead over the half-knot and pass the end of the cord through the ring bead. Then, wrap it around the circle again, following the path of the cord from the previous round. When you get back to the ring bead, thread the cord through it again.

4. *Finish the wreath.* Continue wrapping the foundation circle until you reach the end of the cord, finishing at the ring bead. It will be difficult to feed the cord through the ring bead on the last pass. To make this easier, cut the end of the cord at an angle and compress the cords already threaded through the ring bead as much as you can. Feed the cut cord end through until you can see it on the other side, and then pull it through completely with chain-nose pliers.

5. *Secure the ends.* Weave the cord ends into the middle of the wreath, apply a dab of glue to secure them, and then trim away the excess so you cannot see the cut ends.

6. *Create a second wreath.* Create an additional wreath in the same way.

7. *Create the center wreath.* For the center wreath, string two ring beads onto the leather cord before forming the foundation circle. You will make the center wreath in the same manner as previously, except that you will pass the cord through two ring beads on each round. Position the ring beads opposite each other on the circle.

8. *Create the connectors.* String a bead cap, a glass bead, and another bead cap onto each of the two eye pins and turn simple loops (see page 12) at the ends.

9. *Attach the jump rings.* Open the four 6mm jump rings and feed one through each ring bead on the wreaths by parting the cords to make some room. Do not close the jump rings yet.

10. *Lay out the design.* Lay the three wreaths in a line, placing the double ring bead wreath in the center. Hook the beaded eye pins onto the four jump rings to join the wreaths. Then, close the jump rings.

11. *Complete the bracelet.* Open the 12mm jump rings and attach one to each of the outer wreaths. Add one half of the clasp to each jump ring and then close them.

MATERIALS

- ⅛" (3mm)-wide suede lace, 45" (114.5cm) in each Red, Pink, and White
- 2⅜" (6mm)-diameter silver bracelet memory wire

TOOLS

- Round-nose pliers
- Memory wire shears
- Rotary hand sewing punch
- Scissors
- Needle tool
- Ruler
- Permanent marker

Candy Stripe Bracelet

Finished diameter: about 2" (5cm)

1. Cut the leather pieces. Cut three 13¼" (33.5cm) lengths of each color of suede lace for nine pieces total.

2. Mark the lace. On each lace piece, place a mark ⅛" (3mm) from one end. From the ⅛" (3mm) mark, measure down the center of the lace and place a mark 1" (2.5cm) away from the first mark. Continue marking the lace at 1" (25mm) intervals until you reach the other end of the lace.

3. Punch the holes. Set the hole punch to the smallest setting and carefully line up each mark with the point of the punch. Punch holes along each lace at the marked points.

4. Prepare the wire. Cut one and a half coils from the memory wire. Turn an outward-facing loop (see page 14) on one end. Hold the memory wire in your non-dominant hand and thread on a Red, Pink, and White lace through the first hole of each lace. Thread on the remaining laces in this order. Keep the laces near the threading end of the wire.

5. Loop the first lace. Take the first Red lace (the one farthest from the threading end), pass it in front of the other laces, and thread it back onto the memory wire through the second hole. Make sure the lace does not twist as you do this.

6. Loop the second lace. Take the next lace (the first Pink one) and pass it in front of the hanging laces and beneath the loop created by the Red lace. Thread it onto the memory wire through the second hole.

7. Loop the third lace. Take the next lace (the first White one), pass it in front of the hanging laces, beneath the Pink loop, and thread it onto the wire.

8. Loop the remaining laces. Repeat this process with the remaining laces, making sure you always take the next lace in line. This will create the first twist.

9. Pull the wire through. To continue looping the laces, you will need to pull the wire through the threaded laces. Hold the wire in your non-dominant hand with the threading end pointing upward. Loop the next lace up onto the wire. Using chain-nose pliers in your dominant hand, pull the end of the wire up ¼" (6mm), while pushing the threaded laces down the wire.

5

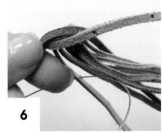

6

7

8

9

12

10. Finish looping the laces. Keep the threading end of the wire facing up and loop the next lace onto it. Pull the wire through the laces with the pliers so the next lace can be added. Sometimes you will need to tug the next lace into position before you can thread it on. Continue adding the laces in this fashion until you have threaded the wire through the last hole of the last lace.

11. Distribute the twists. Push all the twists along the memory wire so they reach the loop at the end. Then, distribute the twists evenly along the wire. Cut the end of the wire to ⅜" (1cm) from the end of the last twist. Turn an outward-facing loop (see page 14).

12. Adjust the laces. Use the needle tool to gently pry out any laces that have become covered by another lace so that all are visible along the bracelet.

- Two 12mm silver disco ball beads
- Two 15mm black Kashmiri beads
- One 16mm black Kashmiri bead
- One 38mm black plastic donut bead (24mm diameter center hole)
- Eight 8/0 clear silver-lined seed beads
- Two 9mm silver end caps (8mm internal diameter)
- 1 silver split ring
- 2 size 2 silver crimp tubes
- 2 silver wire guardians
- 15" (38cm), 0.018", 19-strand silver beading wire
- 1 silver hook and eye clasp
- Sewing thread
- Epoxy adhesive (I used 5 Minute Epoxy)

TOOLS

- Scissors
- Split ring pliers
- Crimping pliers
- Flush cutters
- Toothpick
- Clipboard
- 2 binder clips

MATERIALS

- ⅛" (3mm)-wide suede lace, 60" (152.5cm) in each Black and White
- Two 10mm AB (aurora borealis) crystal helix beads

Licorice Wrap Bracelet

Finished length: 24" (61cm)

Tip

Alternating the colors of the strands will make the two colors appear to twist around the braid. If you'd like the two colors to appear in vertical lines, place the two black pieces together and the two white pieces together before you begin braiding.

1. Cut the lace pieces. Cut two 28" (71cm) lengths of each color of suede lace for four pieces total.

2. Organize the laces. Arrange the lace pieces so the colors alternate. Align the ends and secure them to your work surface (I recommend placing them in the clip of the clipboard).

3. Complete the first braiding step. Starting with the outer left piece (in Position 1), bring it behind the two laces adjacent to it (in Positions 2 and 3).

3

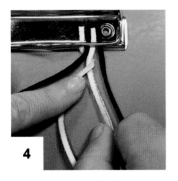

4

5

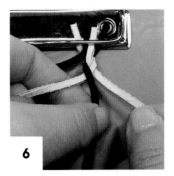

6

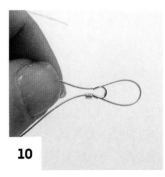

10

11

12

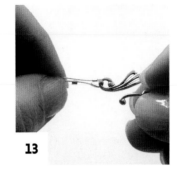

13

4. Complete the second braiding step. Then, bring the working lace back over the front of the lace to the left of it (in Position 2). Always keep the front of the working lace facing the outside as you wrap it to create the round shape.

5. Complete the third braiding step. Starting with the outer right piece (in Position 4), bring it behind the two laces adjacent to it (in Positions 2 and 3).

6. Complete the fourth braiding step. Then, bring the working lace back over the front of the lace to the right of it (in Position 3).

7. Finish the braid. Continue braiding in this manner, bringing the outer laces under two and back over one in the center, alternating left and right sides, until you have reached the ends of the laces. Use binder clips to secure the laces on each end of the braid so it won't unravel. The braid should measure approximately 17½" (44.5cm).

8. Wrap the ends. To secure the braid for use, wrap sewing thread around each end and tie a double knot with it. Trim away the excess lace and thread.

9. Attach the end caps. Mix the epoxy adhesive according to the manufacturer's instructions. Apply enough to the inside of an end cap and to one end of the braid for a secure connection, but not so much the epoxy oozes out when the pieces are connected. Push the end of the braid into the end cap. Repeat for the other end of the braid. Allow the epoxy to set before continuing.

10. Prepare the wire end. Cut a 10" (25.5cm) length of beading wire. String a crimp tube and a wire guardian on one end, threading the end of the beading wire through both holes of the wire guardian.

11. Attach the braid. Thread the beading wire through the end cap loop at one end of the braid, positioning the end cap loop against the wire guardian. Thread the tail end of the beading wire back through the crimp tube and crimp securely.

12. String the beads. String a crystal helix bead, a seed bead, a disco ball bead, a seed bead, a small Kashmiri bead, and a seed bead onto the beading wire. Thread the wire through the first hole of the donut, a seed bead, the large Kashmiri bead, and another seed bead. Thread the wire through the second hole of the donut, and carefully pull the Kashmiri bead into position so it sits flush in the donut center. String the remaining beads in reverse order.

13. Attach the clasp. Repeat Step 10 to thread a crimp tube and wire guardian onto the other end the beading wire. Thread on the hook end of the clasp, positioning it against the wire guardian. Thread the tail end of the wire back through the crimp tube and the first bead of the design. Slide all the beads along the wire toward the braid to remove the slack and then crimp firmly into place. Trim away the excess wire.

14. Complete the bracelet. Open the split ring and use it to connect the other end cap to the second half of the clasp.

Folding and Pleating

Bring an avant-garde touch to your leather jewelry with these bold designs, full of movement and drama. More likely to be seen gracing the fashion runways of New York, these designs are really edgy and fashion forward.

In this section, we'll transform ultra-soft, flexible leathers into knockout statement jewelry with some simple folding and pleating techniques. Combined with a sprinkling of beads and chain, these designs will ramp up your wardrobe. Imagine the comments you'll receive from family and friends about your designer accessories when you wear these bejeweled delights. And we can keep it between you and me that you made them from supplies you picked up at the craft store!

MATERIALS

- Black deertan kidskin
- 1mm round cord, 15" (38cm) in Silver
- Two 20mm antique silver cone ends
- 2 silver eye pins
- 2 size 4 crimp tubes
- 4 size 2 crimp tubes
- Four 4mm silver stardust beads
- 2 silver earring wires

TOOLS

- Round-nose pliers
- Chain-nose pliers
- Flush cutters
- Large crimping pliers for 3mm and larger crimp tubes (I used Beadalon's Mighty Crimper)
- Standard crimping pliers
- Scissors
- Ruler
- Pen
- Rotary hand sewing punch

Midnight Blossoms Earrings

Finished length: 3½" (9cm) from top of earring wire to bottom of stamen

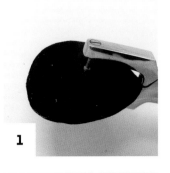

1

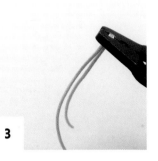

3

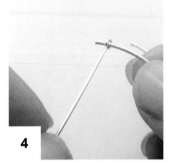

4

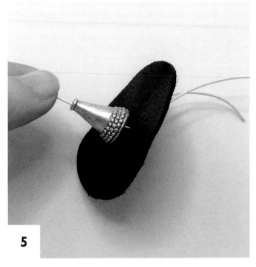

5

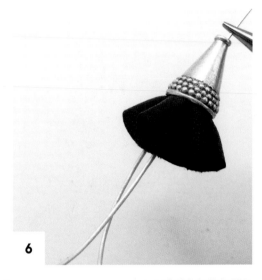

6

1. *Prepare the circle.* Trace a 2⅛" (5.5cm)-diameter circle (I traced around a Sof-Suede lace spool) on the leather and cut it out. Set the hole punch to the smallest setting, find the center of the circle, and punch a hole.

2. *Cut the cords.* Cut one 2½" (6.5cm) and one 2¾" (7cm) stamen from the 1mm cord.

3. *Crimp the cords.* Thread a size 4 crimp tube over the ends of both stamens. After making sure the ends are even, crimp the tube to secure.

4. *Attach the eye pin.* Thread one of the stamens through the loop of an eye pin. Bring the loop up against the crimp tube so the two cords hang down on either side of the loop.

5. *Add the remaining components.* Thread the eye pin through the center of the leather circle and the cone end, threading the wide end of the cone first.

6. *Gather the leather.* Pull the eye pin up firmly to bring the leather and stamens up into the cone. Adjust the leather circle so it is evenly gathered and the stamens are centered beneath it. Create a wrapped loop (see page 13) at the end of the eye pin.

7. *Attach an earring wire.* Open an earring wire and hook it onto the wrapped loop of the eye pin.

8. *Attach the beads.* Cut the ends of the stamens at an angle and string a silver bead onto each. Secure the beads by crimping a size 2 crimp tube onto the end of each stamen.

9. *Make the second earring.* Repeat Steps 1–8 to make a second matching earring.

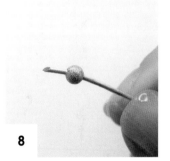

8

MATERIALS

- Gold leather bracelet blank

- Twenty-five 6 x 3mm green tones Czech glass flat rondelles

- Two 13mm green marble lampwork beads

- One 20mm green square lampwork bead

- 1 lime green top-drilled pressed glass leaf bead

- 2 gold flattened head pins

- 5 gold eye pins

- ¾" (2cm)-long fine gold chain

- 15" (38cm), 26-gauge gold wire

- 18" (45.5cm)-long, 9 x 6mm, matte gold oval link chain

- One 6mm gold jump ring

- 1 gold lobster claw clasp

TOOLS

- Flat-nose pliers

- Round-nose pliers

- Chain-nose pliers

- Flush cutters

- Scissors

- Ruler

- Permanent marker

- Rotary hand sewing punch

Green with Envy Necklace

Finished length: 20" (51cm)

   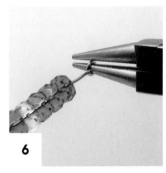

1. Cut the leather. Cut a 4⁵⁄₁₆" (11cm)-wide piece of leather from the bottom of the bracelet blank.

2. Fold the leather. Find the center of the leather by folding it in half, bringing the short edges together with right sides facing.

3. Mark the leather. Open the leather and, on the wrong side, make a mark ⁹⁄₃₂" (0.5cm) on each side of the center fold, approximately ¼" (0.5cm) from the top long edge.

4. Continue marking the leather. Measure out ⁹⁄₁₆" (1.5cm) from the marks made in the previous step, and mark these points. Continue marking at ⁹⁄₁₆" (1.5cm) intervals along the length of the leather.

5. Punch the holes. Set the rotary punch to the smallest setting and punch holes in the leather where marked.

6. Make the dangles. Trim three of the eye pins to 1⁵⁄₈" (4cm) long. String seven rondelles onto each one and turn simple loops (see page 12) at the ends, leaving a consistent gap between the top bead and the loop.

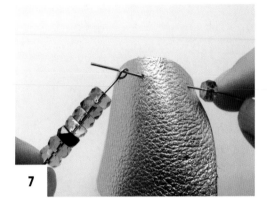

7. Begin attaching the dangles. String a rondelle on an eye pin and thread the eye pin through the first hole in the leather from front to back. Thread it through the second hole from back to front and add one of the beaded eye pin dangles.

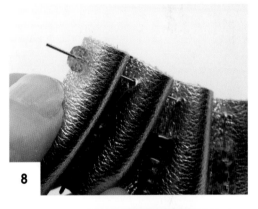

8. Finish attaching the dangles. Keep weaving the eye pin back and forth through the holes in the leather, adding the dangles in the valleys of the pleats. Once the eye pin is threaded through all the holes, string another rondelle on the end and then push the leather along the eye pin until it is neatly pleated. Bend the end at a 45° angle, trim the tail to ⅜" (1cm), and turn a simple loop (see page 12).

9. Create the marble bead dangles. String a rondelle and marble bead on a flat head pin and turn a simple loop (see page 12) at the end. Create a second marble bead component. Attach these to the bottom loops of the two outer dangles.

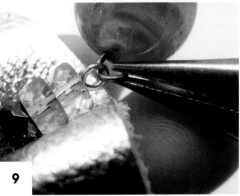

10

10. *Create the center chain.* Thread a rondelle, the square lampwork bead, and another rondelle on an eye pin and turn a simple loop (see page 12) at the end. Attach it to one end of the fine chain. Then, attach the other end of the chain to the bottom loop of the center dangle.

11. *Thread the leaf bead.* Cut a 10" (25cm) length of wire and thread on the leaf bead, leaving a 1½" (4cm) tail.

12. *Position the wire ends.* Bend both wires where they exit the bead holes so they point up toward the top of the leaf. Bend the long wire so it extends directly from the top of the bead, creating a stem.

13. *Wrap the wire.* Wrap the short wire around the stem three times to secure it, and then trim away the excess.

14. *Create a loop.* Make a simple loop (see page 12) above the wire wraps.

15. *Wrap the bead.* Wrap the rest of the wire around the already existing loops on the wire stem and down around the top of the bead until no wire is left.

16. *Attach the leaf bead.* Open the eye pin loop at the bottom of the square bead on the center dangle and attach the wrapped leaf bead.

17. *Complete the necklace.* Cut the oval chain in half and attach one half to each end of the eye pin that was threaded through the leather. Attach the clasp to the other end of one of the chain lengths using jump rings.

12

13

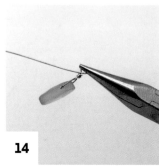

14

15

MATERIALS

- Zebra print leather bracelet blank
- Three 22 x 20mm red rubberized heart beads
- Two 12 x 26mm red howlite teardrop beads
- Two 10 x 25mm ruby sharp oval glass beads
- Three 25mm silver cone-shaped beads
- Eight 25 x 6mm black cylinder beads
- Nineteen 4 x 4.5mm silver spring spacer beads
- One 4mm silver bead cap
- 2 silver wire guardians
- 2 size 2 crimp tubes
- Nine 6mm silver jump rings
- One 70mm silver eye pin
- Seven 50mm silver eye pins
- 3 silver flat head pins
- 8" (20cm)-long, 6 x 9mm, silver textured small and large link oval chain
- 35" (89cm), 26-gauge non-tarnish silver beading wire
- 15" (38cm), 0.012" black beading wire
- 1 silver ball and hitch clasp

TOOLS

- Flat-nose pliers
- Round-nose pliers
- Chain-nose pliers
- Crimping pliers
- Flush cutters
- Scissors
- Rotary hand sewing punch
- Ruler
- Permanent marker

Zebra Ripple Necklace
Finished length: 17½" (44.5cm)

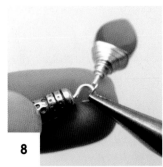

1. Cut the leather. Cut the leather bracelet blank into three ½" (1.5cm)-wide strips the full length of the leather.

2. Punch the holes. Cut one leather piece to half the length. On each half, measure and mark ¼" (6mm) from each end, centering the marks on the width of the leather. Then, starting at the ¼" (6mm) marks, measure and mark at ⅞" (22mm) intervals along the length of each half, centering the marks on the width of the leather. With the rotary punch at the smallest setting, punch a hole at each mark.

3. Start creating the short ribbons. Take one of the short leather pieces and thread a 50mm eye pin through the first hole from front to back. Then, add a spring bead and bring the eye pin through the second hole from back to front.

4. Finish creating the short ribbons. Continue weaving the eye pin in and out of the holes in the leather, adding a bead after each one. Make a simple loop (see page 12) at the end of the eye pin to hold the leather in place. Repeat Steps 3 and 4 with the other short leather piece to create a second ribbon. Set the completed short ribbons aside.

5. Create the long ribbon. Take one of the long strips of leather (set the other piece aside for another project) and mark ⅜" (1cm) from one end, centering the mark on the width of the leather. Then, starting at the ⅜" (1cm) mark, measure and mark at 1³⁄₁₆" (2cm) intervals along the length of the leather. Punch a hole at each mark as before. Repeat Steps 3 and 4 to form a long ribbon from the leather, using the 70mm eye pin.

6. String the beads. Take five eye pins and string cones on three of them and hearts on two of them. Turn simple loops (see page 12) at the ends of the eye pins. String the bead cap and remaining heart on a head pin. String the teardrop beads on the remaining head pins. Turn simple loops (see page 12) on each beaded head pin.

7. Wrap the oval beads. Cut two 16" (40cm) lengths of silver wire. Follow the instructions on pages 16–17 to wrap the tops of the oval beads with the wire.

8. Attach the wrapped beads. Take two of the eye pins threaded with cone beads and open the loops at the narrow ends of the cones. Hook a wrapped bead on each one and close the loops.

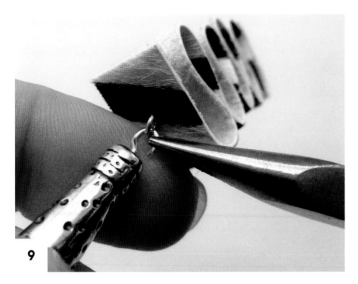

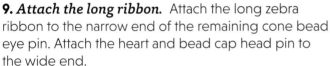

9

13

9. *Attach the long ribbon.* Attach the long zebra ribbon to the narrow end of the remaining cone bead eye pin. Attach the heart and bead cap head pin to the wide end.

10. *Attach the remaining beaded pins.* Open the loops on the two teardrop eye pins and hook one onto each of the smaller zebra ribbons. Connect the other end of each ribbon to the bottom loop of a heart eye pin.

11. *Add jump rings.* Attach a jump ring to the top of each of the five components (three ribbon components, and two cone/wrapped bead components).

12. *Prepare the wire.* Cut 12" (30cm) of black beading wire. Thread a crimp tube onto the wire. Thread the wire end through both holes of the wire guardian and back through the crimp tube. Crimp in place.

13. *Begin stringing the necklace.* String on two cylinder beads. Then, string on one of the cone/wrapped bead components.

14. *Finish stringing the necklace.* Continue stringing the necklace, alternating cylinder beads and beaded components. String the beaded components working from shortest to longest at the center of the necklace, and then back to shortest. Once all the beaded components have been strung, string two cylinder beads. Finish the end of the beading wire with a crimp tube and wire guardian.

15. *Complete the necklace.* Cut the chain into two 4" (10cm) lengths. Attach one length to each end of the beading wire with jump rings. Attach the other ends of the chain to each half of the clasp.

14

Making Beads with Leather

Leather is much more than just a stringing material. Use its flexibility to twist it, roll it, and glue it to create sculptural beads with high visual impact.

Leather and suede lace make equally good choices for creating beads. Try leather trim pieces to make big bold focal beads and use suede lace or leather cord to make colorful, modular components. Each creation will be like a mini 3-D work of art!

MATERIALS

- ³⁄₃₂" (2.5mm)-wide Sof-Suede lace, 100" (254cm) in each Pink, Kiwi, and Light Blue
- Twenty-eight 6mm white glass pearls
- 2⅜" (6cm)-diameter silver memory wire
- Leather adhesive

TOOLS

- Memory wire shears
- Scissors
- Ruler
- Round-nose pliers
- Toothpick

Pastel Disk Bracelet

Finished length: 9⅜" (21.5cm).

Note: The longer length is made to accommodate the disks around your wrist.

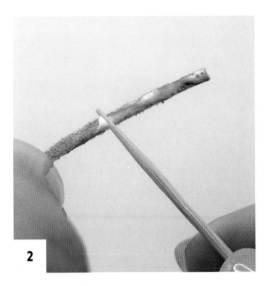

2

Tip

When applied thinly, leather adhesive dries very quickly. Applying a thin layer of the adhesive will give better adhesion than a thick layer, and it will allow the leather to hold together sooner so you can move on to making the next disk.

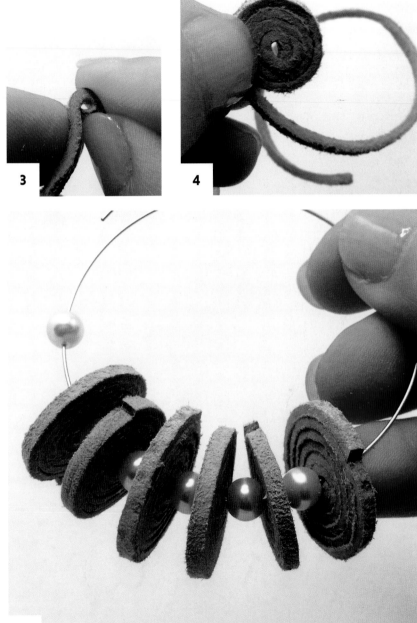

3

4

6

1. Cut the leather pieces. Cut nine 10" (25.5cm) lengths of each color of lace for twenty-seven pieces total.

2. Apply glue. Apply a small amount of adhesive to the end of one piece of lace, on the back, and spread it out thinly with the toothpick.

3. Begin forming the disk bead. Begin to roll the glued end of the lace back on itself, making sure to form a hole for the memory wire.

4. Finish forming the disk bead. Continue applying small amounts of adhesive to the lace, spreading it thinly, and rolling the lace to form a disk until you reach the end.

5. Create the remaining disk beads. Create a disk with each of the remaining lengths of lace.

6. String the bracelet. Make an outward-facing loop at the end of the memory wire. String on a glass pearl followed by a Pink disk bead, a pearl, a Kiwi disk bead, a pearl, a Light Blue disk bead, and another pearl. Continue in this pattern until you have strung all the disks and pearls.

7. Complete the bracelet. Trim the end of the memory wire to ⅜" (1cm) and turn an outward-facing loop.

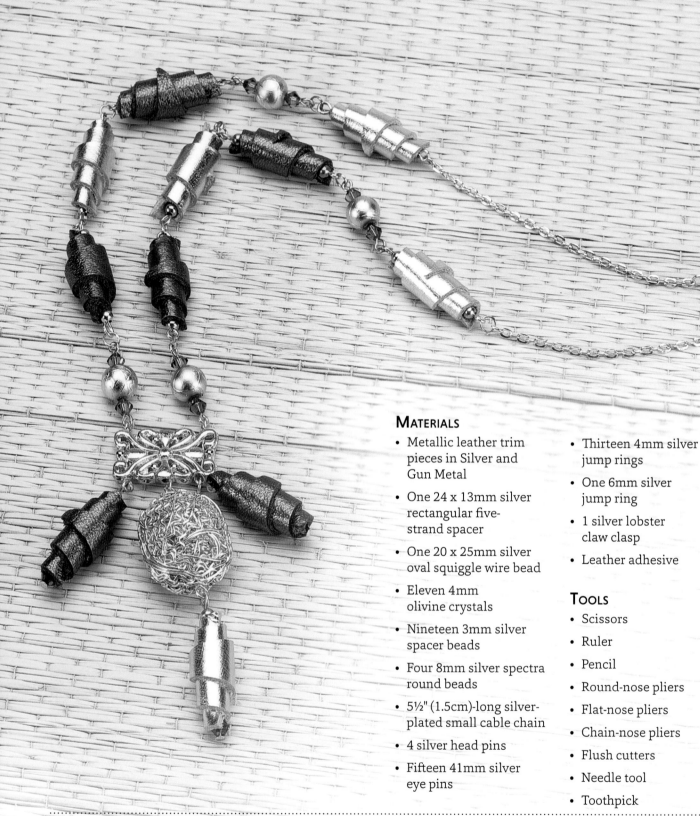

MATERIALS

- Metallic leather trim pieces in Silver and Gun Metal
- One 24 x 13mm silver rectangular five-strand spacer
- One 20 x 25mm silver oval squiggle wire bead
- Eleven 4mm olivine crystals
- Nineteen 3mm silver spacer beads
- Four 8mm silver spectra round beads
- 5½" (1.5cm)-long silver-plated small cable chain
- 4 silver head pins
- Fifteen 41mm silver eye pins
- Thirteen 4mm silver jump rings
- One 6mm silver jump ring
- 1 silver lobster claw clasp
- Leather adhesive

TOOLS

- Scissors
- Ruler
- Pencil
- Round-nose pliers
- Flat-nose pliers
- Chain-nose pliers
- Flush cutters
- Needle tool
- Toothpick

Magic Metals Necklace

Finished length: 21" (53.5cm)

1

2

3

1. Measure and mark the leather. Measure and cut a 2½" (6.5cm)–wide strip the length of the leather from each color of leather. Measure and mark at 1" (2.5cm) intervals along the top long edge of each strip. On the bottom long edge, place a mark ½" (12.5mm) from one side edge and then every 1" (2.5cm) after that. Draw a line from the marks along the top edge to the marks along the bottom edge, creating thin triangles. Measure and mark six Gun Metal and five Silver triangles. Cut them out.

2. Apply adhesive. Working on one triangle at a time, apply adhesive to the back of the leather on the wide edge, leaving the first ¼" (0.5cm) of the edge free of adhesive.

3. Form the beads. Spread the adhesive evenly along the triangle and then roll the leather into a bead, making sure to leave a hole for stringing. Repeat for all the triangles.

4. Create the leather eye pins. String a silver spacer bead, a leather bead, and spacer bead on an eye pin. Turn a simple loop (see page 12) at the end. Create four Silver and four Gun Metal leather eye pins.

5. Create the leather head pins. Take three head pins and string each with an olivine crystal, a leather bead, and a silver spacer bead. Turn simple loops (see page 12) at the ends.

6. String the wire bead. String the silver wire bead on an eye pin and turn a simple loop (see page 12) at the end. You may need to pry the wire strands apart with the needle tool as shown to thread the eye pin through the center of the bead.

7. Attach a leather eye pin. Attach the wire bead eye pin to a Silver leather head pin created in Step 5.

4

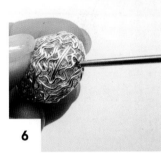
6

7

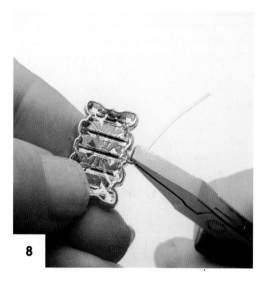

8

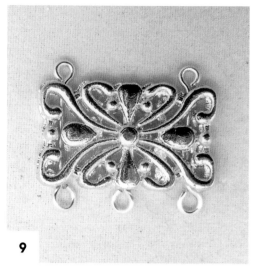

9

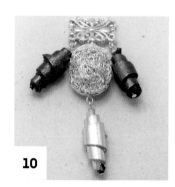

10

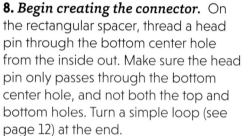

8. Begin creating the connector. On the rectangular spacer, thread a head pin through the bottom center hole from the inside out. Make sure the head pin only passes through the bottom center hole, and not both the top and bottom holes. Turn a simple loop (see page 12) at the end.

9. Finish creating the connector. Thread an eye pin through each of the outer two holes of the connector, passing the pins through both the top and bottom holes, and turn simple loops at the ends.

10. Attach the leather components. Attach the two Gun Metal leather head pins to the outside bottom loops of the connector and the silver wire bead to the middle bottom loop.

11. String the spacer eye pins. On an eye pin, string a crystal, a silver spectra bead, and a crystal. Turn a simple loop (see page 12) at the end. Create four of these spacer components.

12

12. Begin forming the necklace. Attach one of the spacer eye pins to one of the remaining top loops of the connector. Link the other end of the spacer to a Gun Metal leather eye pin with a 4mm jump ring. Then connect a Silver leather eye pin and another Gun Metal leather eye pin in the same way. Attach another spacer eye pin and a Silver leather eye pin with jump rings.

13. Attach the chain. Cut the chain in half and attach the end of one half to the last leather eye pin with a jump ring. Attach the other end to the lobster claw clasp with a jump ring.

14. Finish the necklace. Repeat Steps 12 and 13 to form the other side of the necklace, but finish the chain with the 6mm jump ring.

MATERIALS

- Metallic leather trim piece in Gold

- Three 7 x 10mm purple faceted crystal rondelles

- One 10 x 18mm purple faceted crystal rondelle

- One 15 x 20mm amethyst beaded bead

- Assorted seed beads in gold, silver, black, and purple (I used a packet of Bead Gravy Caviar Blend beads [BDGR-33])

- One 12 x 14mm white-and-gold cloisonné bead

- 2 gold beveled crystal rondelles

- Two 12 x 17mm gold four-petal filigree bead caps

- 25" (63.5cm), 28-gauge gold beading wire

- 20" (51cm), 22-gauge gold beading wire

- 10" (25.5cm), 20-gauge gold beading wire

- 14" (35.5cm)-long, 6 x 8mm, matte gold oval chain

- Hollow plastic jewelry tube

- Crystal-encrusted clasp

- Leather adhesive

TOOLS

- Scissors
- Ruler
- Pencil
- Round-nose pliers
- Flat-nose pliers
- Chain-nose pliers
- Flush cutters
- 2 bead stoppers
- Thick bamboo skewer or size 6 knitting needle
- Toothpick

Gold and Purple Tube Necklace
Finished length: 23" (58.5cm)

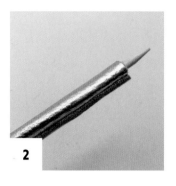

2

3

4

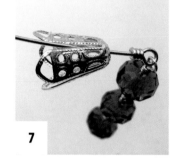

7

8

1. *Cut the leather.* Measure, mark, and cut a 1½" (4cm)-wide strip the length of the leather trim piece.

2. *Form the tube.* Place the knitting needle against the long edge of the leather and roll the leather once around the needle. Run a bead of adhesive along the edge of the leather roll and spread it evenly across the unrolled leather with the toothpick. Continue rolling the leather around itself to form a tube, keeping it in place until the adhesive holds. Set the leather tube aside to dry.

3. *Create a wrapped-loop bead.* Cut a 3" (7.5cm) length of 22-gauge wire. String on a small rondelle and move it to the middle of the wire. Place the jaws of the chain-nose pliers against the bead and bend the wire at a 45° angle. Remove the bead and create a wrapped loop (see page 13). String the bead back on and create a wrapped loop at the other end of the bead.

4. *Attach additional beads.* Cut another 3" (7.5cm) length of 22-gauge wire. Thread another small rondelle along to the middle of the wire and bend the wire at a 45° angle as before. Remove the bead. Create a loop at the bend. Hook the loop through a wrapped loop of the first rondelle and complete the wrap. String the second rondelle back on the wire and create a wrapped loop (see page 13). Connect a third rondelle in the same way.

5. *Create and attach additional beads.* Cut two 3½" (8.5cm) lengths of 22-gauge wire. Following Steps 3 and 4, use one piece to make a wrapped-loop bead with the beaded amethyst bead. Use the remaining piece to make a wrapped-loop cloisonné bead, attaching it to the beaded amethyst bead as before.

6. *Prepare the beading wire.* Cut 8" (20.5cm) of 20-gauge wire. Create a wrapped loop (see page 13) at one end, connecting it to the three joined wrapped-loop rondelles before closing the loop.

7. *Begin stringing the necklace.* String on a bead cap. Cut 3" (7.5cm) of plastic tubing and thread it onto the wire.

8. *String the leather tube.* Slide the leather tube bead onto the beading wire over the tubing and add another bead cap. Adjust the petals of the bead caps so they fit snugly around the leather tube ends. Help shape the necklace by bringing the leather tube bead into a gentle curve.

9. *String the rondelles.* String a beveled rondelle, the large purple rondelle, and the second beveled rondelle onto the wire.

10. *Attach the remaining wrapped-loop beads.* Create a wrapped loop at the end of the necklace, attaching it to the wrapped-loop cloisonné bead before closing.

11. *String the seed beads.* Cut a 21" (53.5cm) length of 26-gauge wire. Attach a bead stopper to one end and then thread on 12" (30.5cm) of seed beads. Attach another bead stopper to keep the beads in place.

12. *Begin forming the wrap.* Move the beads to within 3" (7.5cm) of one end of the wire. Wrap the beaded wire once around the leather tube at the amethyst rondelle end, near the bead cap. Remove the bead stopper and thread the short end of the wire back through several beads. Take care not to kink the wire as you pull it through. Wrap the short end of the wire around the leather twice and thread it through several more beads before cutting away the excess.

13. *Finish forming the wrap.* Continue wrapping the beaded wire around the leather.

14. *Secure the wrap.* To end the wrap, remove the bead stopper and thread the end of the wire back through the previous coil of beads. Wrap the wire around the leather again and thread it through the next coil of beads. Wrap the wire around the leather twice and thread it through more beads. Trim away the excess.

15. *Complete the necklace.* Cut the chain into two 7" (18cm) lengths. Attach one length to each end of the necklace by opening the end link of the chain. Attach each half of the clasp to the other ends of the chain pieces.

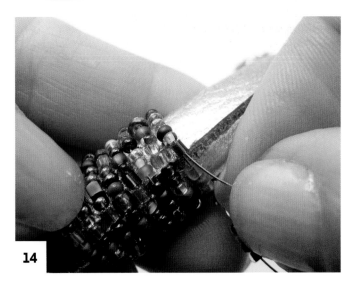

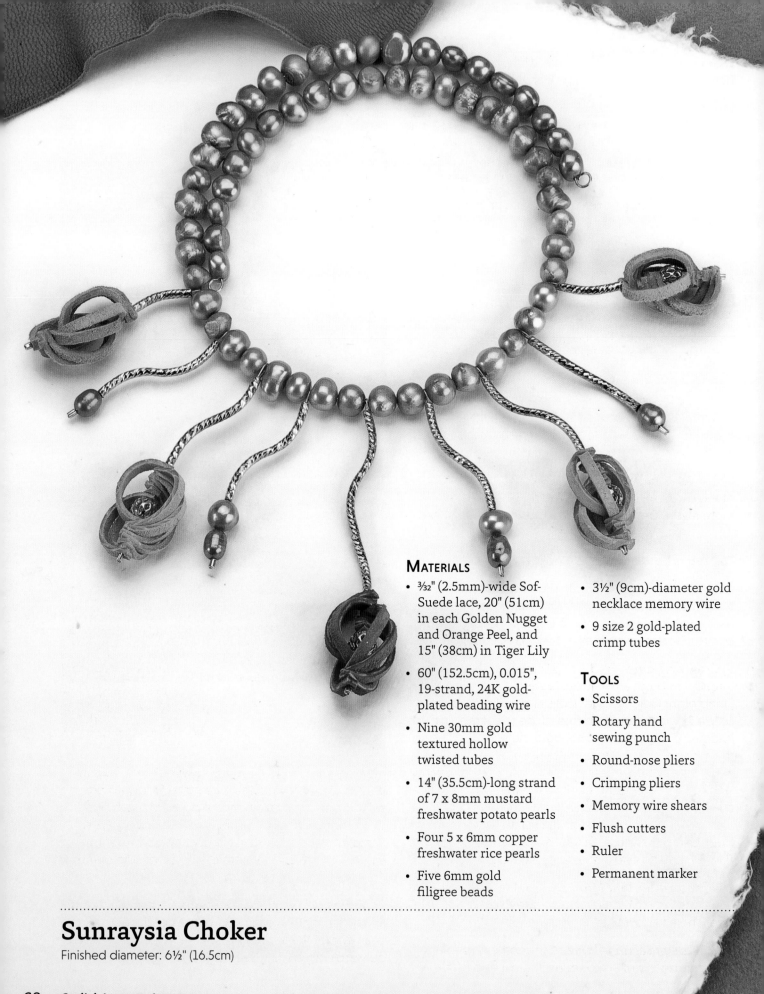

MATERIALS

- ³⁄₃₂" (2.5mm)-wide Sof-Suede lace, 20" (51cm) in each Golden Nugget and Orange Peel, and 15" (38cm) in Tiger Lily
- 60" (152.5cm), 0.015", 19-strand, 24K gold-plated beading wire
- Nine 30mm gold textured hollow twisted tubes
- 14" (35.5cm)-long strand of 7 x 8mm mustard freshwater potato pearls
- Four 5 x 6mm copper freshwater rice pearls
- Five 6mm gold filigree beads
- 3½" (9cm)-diameter gold necklace memory wire
- 9 size 2 gold-plated crimp tubes

TOOLS

- Scissors
- Rotary hand sewing punch
- Round-nose pliers
- Crimping pliers
- Memory wire shears
- Flush cutters
- Ruler
- Permanent marker

Sunraysia Choker

Finished diameter: 6½" (16.5cm)

1. Cut the lace pieces. Cut eight 1⅛" (3cm) pieces of Tiger Lily lace. Cut sixteen 1⅛" (3cm) pieces of each Gold Nugget and Orange Peel lace.

2. Punch the holes. Measure and mark ¹⁄₁₆" (2mm) from each end of all the lace pieces. Set the rotary punch to the smallest setting and punch a hole at each mark, taking care to center the holes along the leather.

3. Cut the beading wire. Cut the following lengths of beading wire: Two 5" (12.5cm) pieces, four 6" (15cm) pieces, two 7" (18cm) pieces, and one 8" (20.5cm) piece.

4. Create a ray. Begin with a 5" (12.5cm) length of beading wire. Fold it in half, forming a round loop at the center, and thread the ends through a hollow tube. Slide the tube up the beading wire, leaving a small loop at the top. String a copper pearl and a crimp tube onto the wire ends.

5. Secure the ray. Crimp the tube securely in place and trim away the excess beading wire. Repeat with the second 5" (12.5cm) length of beading wire to make another ray.

6. Continue making the rays. Working with two of the 6" (15cm) lengths of beading wire, create two more rays as before, but add a mustard pearl before the copper pearl.

7. Cut a tube to size. Take a hollow tube and carefully cut it in half with the flush cutters.

8. Shape the cut ends. Place the flattened cut end of each tube into the outer hole of the crimping pliers and reshape them so they are round again.

9. Create a flame. Fold a 6" (15cm) wire in half and thread it through a half tube, leaving a loop as before. String eight Gold Nugget laces and a filigree bead onto the wire ends. Then thread the tail of the first lace (the one closest to the tube) onto the wire ends. Take the second lace and thread its tail onto the beading wire, making sure it passes in front of the first lace, but behind the other laces. Continue in this fashion until all the tails have been looped onto the wire. String on a crimp tube and push it up against the laces so they bow. Crimp to secure. Fan all the pieces out to form a flame shape. Create a second Gold Nugget flame.

10. Create additional flames. Use the 7" (18cm) pieces of wire to create two Orange Peel flames, using one whole hollow tube for each one.

11. Create the center flame. Cut another tube in half and use the pliers to round the cut end of the

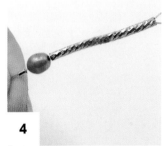

2

4

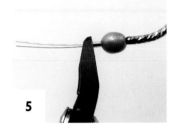

5

7

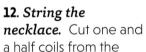

8

9

tube as before. String a whole tube and the half tube on the folded 8" (20.5cm) length of wire so the bend in the tubes continues. Then, create a Tiger Lily flame.

12. String the necklace. Cut one and a half coils from the memory wire using the memory wire shears. Thread the components onto the wire in the following order, stringing two mustard pearls in between each one: Gold Nugget flame, copper pearl ray, Orange Peel flame, mustard and copper pearl ray, and Tiger Lily flame. Continue the pattern on the other side of the necklace in reverse order.

12

13. Finish the necklace. Divide the remaining pearls and thread half on each side of the necklace. Trim each end of the memory wire to ⅜" (1cm) and turn an outward-facing loop (see page 14).

Creating Links, Chains, and Connectors

Connecting jewelry components together with jump rings and metal chain is the basis of all jewelry making, but let's turn that notion upside down, switch out the chain, and introduce leather links to create a softer, more tactile, connection. It's a classy substitute that will give your jewelry a chic, designer look.

In this section, we'll use a little creative engineering to form giant chains of leather cord, short colorful suede lace connectors, and safari-inspired links. Each one will bring that *wow* factor to your finished piece.

MATERIALS

- Leopard print leather bracelet blank
- Three 25 x 25mm brown shell beads with 15 x 15mm openings
- Six 16mm ribbon clamps
- Four 4mm silver jump rings
- 1 silver ball and hitch clasp

TOOLS

- Flat-nose pliers
- Chain-nose pliers
- Scissors
- Ruler
- Pen

Leopard Print Link Bracelet
Finished length: 8" (20cm)

2

3

1. *Cut the leather pieces.* Cut two 9⁄16" (1.5cm)-wide strips the length of the leather. Cut six 2" (5cm)-long pieces from the two strips.

2. *Loop the leather.* Fold a leather piece over one end of a shell bead and line up the two leather ends. Place a ribbon clamp over the leather ends and gently squeeze the teeth with the flat-nose pliers until the leather is secure.

3. *Loop the next piece.* Fold another piece of leather over the other end of the shell bead and secure it with a ribbon clamp as before. Create two more sets of shell/leather links in the same way.

4. *Finish the bracelet.* Connect the links with jump rings. Then, add a jump ring to each end link, adding one half of the clasp to each before closing.

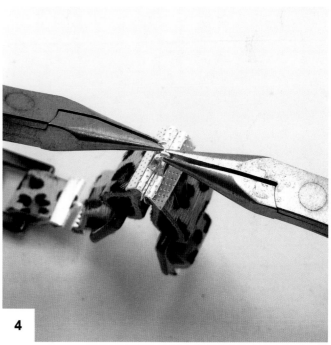

4

MATERIALS

- ³⁄₃₂" (2.5mm)-wide Sof-Suede lace, 5" (12.5cm) in Aqua
- ⅛" (0.5cm)-wide suede lace, 5" (12.5cm) in Turquoise
- Sixteen 4mm faceted mint alabaster AB (aurora borealis) rounds
- 2 blue lampwork flower beads
- Two 3mm silver beads
- Eight 6mm silver ribbon clamps
- ⅞" (22mm)-diameter silver ring-size memory wire
- Two 50mm silver head pins
- 2 silver earring wires
- Ten 4mm silver jump rings
- Hollow jewelry tubing

TOOLS

- Scissors
- Flat-nose pliers
- Round-nose pliers
- Chain-nose pliers
- Memory wire shears
- Flush cutters
- Ruler
- Permanent marker

Turquoise Flower Drop Earrings

Finished length: 3½" (9cm)

1

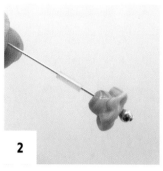

2

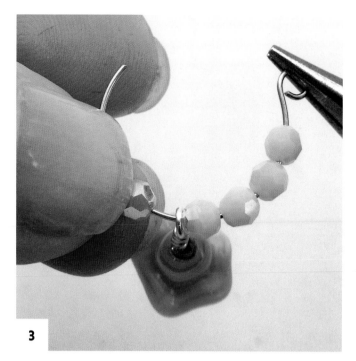

3

1. Cut the memory wire. Cut a coil from the memory wire using the memory wire shears. Cut away ⅜" (1cm) from one end. Turn an outward-facing loop on one end.

2. Create the flower dangle. Cut a length of tubing to fit inside the flower bead. String a silver bead, the flower bead, and the tubing onto a head pin and make a wrapped loop (see page 13) at the end.

3. Create the beaded loop. String four crystals, the flower dangle, and four additional crystals onto the end of the memory wire loop. Turn another outward-facing loop (see page 14) at the end.

4. Create the leather connectors. Cut two 1⅜" (3.5cm) lengths of each color of lace for four pieces total. Take one lace of each color, line up the ends, and place them inside a ribbon clamp. Secure in place with flat-nose pliers. Line up the opposite ends, place them in a clamp, and secure in place. Repeat with the second pair of laces to make a second connector.

5. Attach the beaded loop. Attach one end of the beaded loop to one of the leather connector ribbon clamps with a jump ring. Attach the remaining leather connector to the other end of the beaded loop with a jump ring.

6. Finish the earring. Attach a jump ring to the free end of each leather connector. Open a third jump ring, and hook on the two leather connector jump rings just added, and an earring wire.

7. Make the second earring. Repeat Steps 1–6 to make a second matching earring.

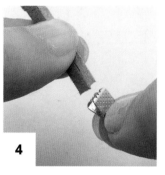

4

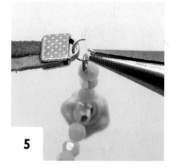

5

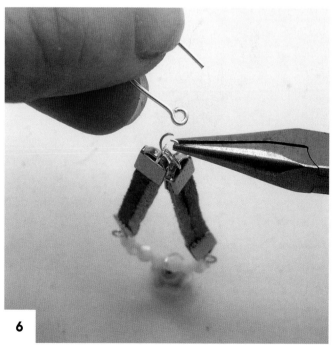

6

MATERIALS

- 1mm round leather cord, 40" (101.5cm) in each Bronze, Gold, and Silver
- Five 17 x 20mm wire beads
- 1 silver teardrop component with light topaz crystal
- 45 size 4 silver-plated crimp tubes
- Twenty 6mm silver jump rings
- Silver toggle clasp

TOOLS

- Scissors
- Ruler
- Large crimping pliers for 3mm and larger crimp tubes (I used Beadalon's Mighty Crimper)
- Chain-nose pliers
- Needle tool
- Permanent marker

Note: Instructions note the ring sizes as the length of lace required to create the rings and not the finished diameter.

Leather Chain Necklace

Finished length: 17½" (44.5cm)

1. Cut the leather pieces. Cut seven 3" (7.5cm) lengths, two 2½" (6.5cm) lengths, and two 2" (5cm) lengths of each of the three colors of round leather cord (33 pieces total).

2. Begin forming the circles. Begin with one 3" (7.5cm) leather piece of each color. Slide a crimp tube onto one end of each one. Then, form them into circles by bringing the other end into the crimp tube, making sure that both ends are flush with ends of the tube. (Note: For ease, the photo shows the leather ends extended past the ends of the crimp tube.)

3. Crimp the circles. Crimp the circles in place, positioning the fold of the crimp tube so it faces into the circle.

4. Thread the circles. Take another 3" (7.5cm) length of cord and string all three completed circles onto it. Slide on a crimp tube, and form the new cord into a circle as before. Crimp to secure. Repeat with cords in the remaining two colors so you have a set of three circles linked to another set of three circles. Repeat again to add a third set of three circles to the chain. Set these aside.

5. Complete the circles. Form all the remaining lengths of cord into individual circles, following Steps 2–3.

6. Mark the cord. Measure 1½" (4cm) along one end of a remaining length of cord and mark it with a marker. Repeat for the remaining two colors of cord.

7. Form the circles. Thread on a crimp tube. Then, feed the short end of the cord back into the crimp tube from the same side, forming a circle. Adjust the size of the circle until the mark is at the edge of the crimp tube. Repeat for the remaining two colors of cord.

8. Crimp the circles. Crimp the circles in place, and then carefully trim away the excess cord. Create two circles of this size in each color for six total. Then, create two sets of 1" (2.5cm) rings in each color in the same way.

9. Make the graduated chain. Collect the individual circles you created in Steps 5–8. Divide them into groups of three according to size, with one of each color in every group. You will have 1" (2.5cm), 1½" (4cm), 2" (5cm), 2½" (6.5cm), and 3" (7.5cm) circles. Connect five circle sets of each size together with jump rings to form a graduated chain going from smallest to largest. Create a matching chain for the other side of the necklace with the remaining circles.

10. Form the holes. Using the needle tool, create holes in the two corners diagonal from each other in each wire bead.

11. Attach the graduated chains. Connect a 3" (7.5cm) ring set from a graduated chain to a corner of a wire bead using a jump ring. Repeat to attach the remaining graduated chain to a wire bead.

12. Attach another circle set. Using jump rings, connect an individual set of 3" (7.5cm) circles to the other end of the wire beads with the graduated chains attached. Then, connect another wire bead to each of the individual 3" (7.5cm) circle sets.

13. Join the ends. Finally, join the two sides of the necklace together by connecting each end of the chain with three 3" (76mm) circle sets to the wire beads on the ends of the necklace halves.

14. Create the focal piece. Attach a jump ring to each hole in the remaining wire bead. Connect one jump ring to the center circle set of the necklace, and the other to the silver teardrop component.

15. Finish the necklace. Connect one half of the toggle clasp to each end of the necklace.

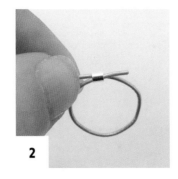

2

3

4

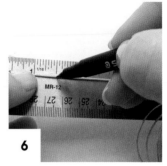

6

7

Tip

For added security, you can add a drop of craft cement inside the crimp tube.

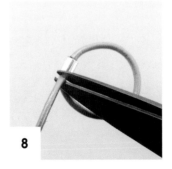

8

9

10

11

Coloring and Die Cutting Leather

Are you a fan of black clothing? We all know that black clothing pieces are wardrobe staples, but let's face it, on its own, black can be boring! As a color aficionado, I'm here to shake up your love of black a bit and encourage you to breathe some excitement into your wardrobe by adding a pop of color to it!

In this section we'll take plain black leather, dress it up with shimmery paint, and turn it into some whimsical and artsy pieces of jewelry that are worthy of placement in a gallery. In other words, we're going to make black *fun*!

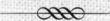

MATERIALS

- Black leather wristband
- Three 36mm gold filigree squares
- Four 32mm gold filigree circles
- 9½" (24cm)-long gold hammered 14mm circle chain
- 1 gold toggle clasp
- Fourteen 6mm gold jump rings
- Metallic paint for leather in Hi Lite Blue
- Drywall mesh joint tape (self-adhesive)

TOOLS

- Stiff bristle paintbrush
- Flush cutters
- Chain-nose pliers
- Flat-nose pliers
- Craft knife
- Metal-edged ruler
- Scissors

Cleopatra Necklace
Finished length: 6½" (16.5cm)

1. Prepare the leather. Cut a 4½" (11.5cm) piece of drywall mesh joint tape and apply it to one end of the leather wristband on the front side. Make sure there are no gaps between the tape and the leather surface to keep the paint from seeping under the tape.

2. Apply the paint. Dip the dry brush tip into the metallic paint and dab it onto a scrap of paper to remove the excess. Touch the brush to the surface of the leather repeatedly over the entire area covered by the tape. Make the paint application as even as possible. Reload the brush if necessary. Allow the paint to dry.

3. Cut the leather squares. Remove the mesh and cut the stenciled portion of the leather into three 1 5/16" (3.5cm) squares with the craft knife.

4. Begin shaping the filigree squares. Grip one corner of a filigree square (with the wrong side facing up) and bend it at a 90° angle at the last scallop. Repeat on all four corners.

5. Finish shaping the filigree squares. Use your fingers to continue rolling each corner until it forms an angle just less than 180° to the rest of the square. Repeat Steps 4–5 for the remaining filigree squares.

6. Place the squares. Fit a leather square into a filigree square, tucking two of the leather edges under two of the folded corners. Place the third leather edge under a corner, allowing the leather to puff up at the center of the square. Repeat for the fourth edge.

7. Create the additional square components. Create two more leather and filigree squares in the same way.

8. Attach jump rings. Slide jump rings through the bases of two filigree corners on opposite sides of two square components. On the remaining square component, attach jump rings at the bases of two adjacent corners. Attach jump rings on opposite sides of each filigree circle.

9. Connect the filigree components. Using the jump rings, connect the filigree squares and circles, alternating the pattern. Place the square with the adjacent jump rings in the center, forming a pattern of circle, square, circle, adjacent square, circle, square, circle.

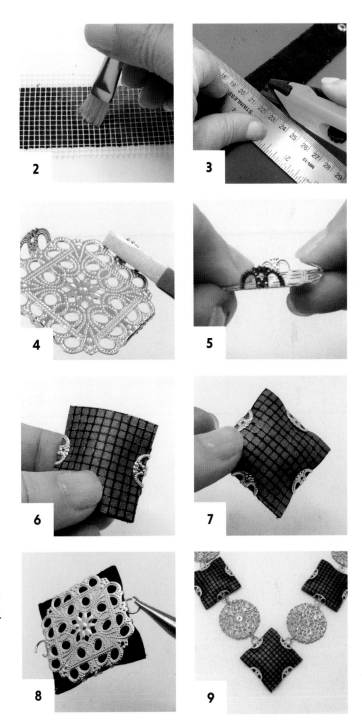

10. Attach the chain. Cut the chain in half and attach one half to each end of the necklace.

11. Finish the necklace. Using the small link at each end of the chain, connect one half of the clasp to each end of the necklace.

- 10" (25.5cm), 20-gauge silver non-tarnish beading wire
- 20" (51cm)-long black polyester chain
- Two 6mm black jump rings
- 1 black toggle and clasp set

Tools
- Scissors
- Stiff bristle paintbrush
- Flat-nose pliers
- Chain-nose pliers
- Round-nose pliers
- Rotary hand sewing punch
- Flush cutters
- Ruler
- Permanent marker

Materials
- Black deertan kidskin
- Metallic paint for leather in Pearlescent Magenta, Pearlescent Turquoise, and Metallic Bronze
- 15mm striped hollow glass beads, one in each amethyst, blue, and brown
- Four 4mm black bicone glass beads

Seed Pod Necklace
Finished length: 21¼" (54cm)

2

3

4

5

1. Cut the leather pieces. Cut three 1¼" (3cm) squares of leather.

2. Paint the squares. Paint each of the three squares with a light coat of paint, using a different color for each one. When dry, add a second light coat of paint. Allow all of the pieces to dry before continuing.

3. Punch the holes. On the front of the leather squares, measure ¼" (0.5cm) in from one corner and place a mark. Make another mark ¼" (0.5cm) in from the diagonal corner. Repeat on the remaining leather squares. Set the hole punch to the smallest hole and punch the holes in the corners where marked.

4. Attach the chain. Cut a 6" (15cm) length of wire and two 8¾" (22cm) lengths of polyester chain. Create a wrapped loop (see page 13) at one end of the wire, but before wrapping the wire around the stem, hook the last link of one half of the chain onto the wire.

6

5. Begin stringing the necklace. Slide a black bead, one corner of the Metallic Bronze square, the brown bead, and the other corner of the Metallic Bronze square onto the wire. Next, add the Pearlescent Turquoise square and blue bead, and then the Pearlescent Magenta square and amethyst bead, stringing a black bead between each square. Finish with a black bead.

6. Attach the chain. Slide the beads and leather squares along the wire to the looped end, making sure there are no gaps between them, and create a wrapped loop (see page 13) at the other end of the wire. Before wrapping the wire around the stem, hook on the other half of the polyester chain.

7. Shape the wire. Help shape the necklace by bringing the wire into a gentle curve.

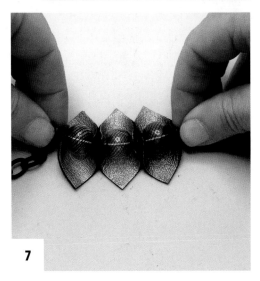
7

8. Finish the necklace. Attach a jump ring to the end of each chain and add one half of the clasp to each side of the necklace.

MATERIALS

- Black deertan kidskin
- Small black leather knot bead
- Thirteen 4mm AB (aurora borealis) crystal bicones
- 1 silver ball head pin
- 35" (89cm), 26-gauge silver non-tarnish artistic wire
- Metallic paint for leather in Pearlescent White
- E6000 adhesive
- Adjustable silver filigree ring base

TOOLS

- Scissors
- Circle template measuring 2⅛" (5.5cm) in diameter (a Sof-Suede lace spool makes a good template)
- Round-nose pliers
- Flat-nose pliers
- Flush cutters
- Paintbrush
- Butane lighter
- Rotary hand sewing punch
- Bead stopper
- Permanent marker

Floral Ring

Finished width: 2" (5cm) in diameter

1. Cut the circle. Trace around the circle template on the leather and cut out the circle.

2. Create the flower. Trim the edges of the circle to form a flower shape.

3. Apply the paint. Paint the leather with a light coat of paint, leaving a narrow border along all the edges unpainted. Allow it to dry. Paint the flower with a second light coat of paint and allow it to dry completely before continuing.

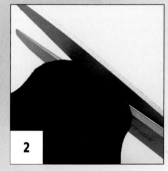

4. Shape the leather. Light the butane lighter and hold the leather with the pliers. With the painted side facing the flame, slowly move the flame backward and forward along the edge of one petal until it begins to cup. Rotate the flower and continue applying heat with the flame until all the petals have cupped.

5. Punch the center hole. Set the hole punch to the second smallest setting and punch a hole in the center of the flower.

6. Prepare the wire. Cut a 30" (76cm) length of wire. Place a bead stopper on one end, and string on twelve crystals.

7. Move a bead. Slide the last crystal added to the wire to within 2" (5cm) of the free end. Bend the wire at both holes of the bead, and bring the wires together at the front of the bead. Pinch them together.

8. Secure the bead. Twist the wires around each other by holding the bead with one hand and the wire with the other hand, approximately ¾" (2cm) from the bead. Turn the bead until the wires are twisted tightly together and you have formed a stamen.

9. Move the second bead. Slide the second crystal along the wire to about ¾" (2cm) from the end of the twisted wire. Bend the wire at both holes of the bead as before and twist to create a second stamen. Repeat with all the beads on the wire to form twelve stamens.

10. Shape the stamens. Once the last stamen has been formed, twist the loose wire ends together twice. Distribute the stamens evenly in a circle, and cup them slightly.

11. Attach the flower center. On the head pin, string a crystal and the leather knot bead. Place the end of the head pin through the middle of the twisted stamens and then through the hole in the leather flower. Trim the wire ends to 1" (2.5cm). Wrap them into a coil and flatten it against the bottom of the flower. (Note: For ease, the coil is shown here without the leather attached.)

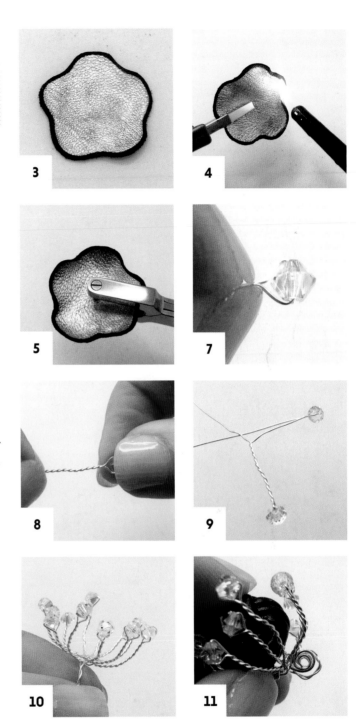

12. Finish the ring. Apply a generous amount of adhesive to the ring base and attach it to the leather flower.

MATERIALS

- Black leather wristband (quantities are for medium-size bracelet)
- Black deertan kidskin
- Metallic paint for leather in Pearlescent Magenta
- Nineteen 6mm black rounds
- 4 black seed beads
- Leather adhesive
- Black sewing thread
- Scrap of cardstock

TOOLS

- Paintbrush
- Rotary hand sewing punch
- Pliers
- Scissors
- Ruler
- Permanent marker
- Needle
- Die cutting machine
- Die for 1" (2.5cm) circles
- ⅝" (1.5cm) paper punch
- Butane lighter

Shimmering Coral Bracelet
Finished size: 2½" (6.5cm) internal diameter

Tip

Some projects call for a die cutting machine and dies, which can be pricey. If desired, you can cut the circles and rings required for these projects by hand. Use a compass to draw templates from cardstock, and then trace them onto the leather.

3

4

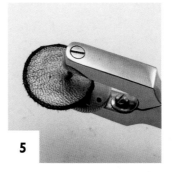

5

6

7

8

1. *Create a template.* Punch the cardstock with the paper punch to create a template.

2. *Trace the template.* Trace around the inside of the template on the back of a piece of kidskin leather to create four ⅝" (1.5cm) circles. Cut out the circles.

3. *Die cut the circles.* Cut two pieces of leather measuring approximately 5½" x 6" (14 x 15cm) to fit the die. Place one piece of leather, grain side down, over the die, and then sandwich everything between the two cutting pads. Place the cutting pads with leather and die on the bed of the die cutting machine with the leather facing up. Crank the handle to move the die through the roller (be sure to follow the manufacturer's instructions for your particular machine). Repeat with the second piece of leather and remove all the die-cut 1" (2.5cm) circles from the leather. You will need approximately nineteen circles total for the bracelet. Set four aside for the matching earrings (see page 88).

4. *Paint the circles.* Paint the front of each circle with two light coats of paint, leaving a narrow border unpainted all the way around the edges. Allow the circles to dry between applications and to dry completely before continuing.

5. *Punch the holes.* Set the rotary punch to the smallest setting and punch two holes in the center of each circle. like a button. For the die-cut circles, place the holes approximately ¼" (0.5cm) apart. For the smaller circles, punch the holes approximately ⅛" (3mm) apart.

6. *Shape the leather.* Light the butane lighter and hold one circle with the pliers. With the painted side facing the flame, place the edge of the circle in the flame until it begins to curl up, taking care that it does not burn. Rotate the circle and repeat all the way around the edge until the entire circle is slightly cupped. Repeat with the remaining circles.

7. *Stitch the beads.* Thread the needle with a comfortable length of black thread. Take one of the circles with the holes in the center and pass the needle through one of the holes from back to front, leaving a 2" (5cm) tail. Thread on a bead and pass the needle through the other hole from front to back. Tie a double knot and repeat, bringing the needle through to the front of the circle, through the bead, and out to the back again. Tie the thread off in a double knot and trim the ends. Sew seed beads onto the small circles and 6mm rounds onto the large circles.

8. *Attach the circles.* Glue each of the circles onto the leather wristband, slightly overlapping the edges. Place the smaller ones in any gaps.

MATERIALS

- Black deertan kidskin
- Metallic paint for leather in Pearlescent Magenta, Halo Pink Gold, and Super Copper
- Four 6mm black rounds
- 4 black seed beads
- Leather adhesive
- Black sewing thread
- Scrap of cardstock
- 2 black earring wires
- Four 6mm black jump rings
- Two 4mm black jump rings
- 2 black head pins

TOOLS

- ¼" (0.5cm) flat paintbrush
- Rotary hand sewing punch
- Round-nose pliers
- Chain-nose pliers
- Flush cutters
- Scissors
- Marker or pen
- Die cutting machine
- Die for 1" (2.5cm) circles
- Paper punches in ⅝" (1.5cm) and 1½" (4cm)
- Needle
- Butane lighter

Shimmering Coral Earrings

Finished length: 4⅛" (10.5cm)

Caution!

Proper care must be exercised when using a flame to manipulate the shape of leather. While leather is flame-resistant (in fact it is used in firefighters' uniforms) it will get hot and give off an odor. Use pliers to hold the leather to keep your hands away from the flame, and work in a well-ventilated space.

1. Create the templates. Punch the cardstock with each of the paper punches to create two templates.

2. Trace the templates. On the back of the kidskin leather, trace around the inside of the templates to create two 1 ½" (4cm) circles and four ⅝" (1.5cm) circles. Cut the circles out. You will also need four of the 1" (2.5cm) circles leftover from the matching bracelet (see page 86), or die cut them.

3. Paint the circles. Paint each of the circles with two light coats of paint, leaving a narrow border unpainted all around the edges. Allow the coats to dry between applications. Paint the 1 ½" (4cm) circles and two of the 1" (2.5cm) circles Pearlescent Magenta; paint two 1" (2.5cm) and two ⅝" (1.5cm) circles Halo Pink Gold; and paint the two remaining ⅝" (1.5cm) circles with Super Copper. Allow all paint to dry before continuing.

4. Shape the leather. When dry, light the butane lighter and hold the edge of one circle with the pliers (painted side facing the flame). Place the edge of the circle in the flame until it begins to curl up. It will take just a few seconds, so take care that it does not burn. Rotate the circle and repeat all the way around the edge until it is slightly cup-shaped. Do the same for all the circles.

5. Punch the holes. Set the rotary punch to the second smallest setting and punch a hole ¹⁄₁₆" (2mm) from the edge at the top and bottom of the following: two 1 ½" (4cm) circles, two 1" (2.5cm) Halo Pink Gold circles, and two ⅝" (1.5cm) Super Copper circles.

6. Connect the circles. Divide the circles into two sets of three, with one circle of each size in each set. Connect the circles in each set together with 6mm jump rings, forming a graduated chain.

7. Attach a bead. String a 6mm bead on a head pin and turn a simple loop (see page 12). Attach it to the bottom of the smallest circle in one chain with a 4mm jump ring. Attach the top of the largest circle to the loop of an earring wire. Repeat for the second chain of circles.

8. Punch the holes. Set the jewelry punch to the smallest setting and punch two holes, like buttonholes, in the center of smallest circle in each chain and in each of the remaining circles. For the 1" (2.5cm) circles, place the holes approximately ¼" (0.5cm) apart. For the ⅝" (1.5cm) circles, punch the holes approximately ⅛" (3mm) apart.

9. Stitch the beads. Thread the needle with a comfortable length of black thread. Take one of the circles with the holes in the center and pass the needle through one of the holes from back to front, leaving a 2" (5cm) tail. Thread on a bead and pass the needle through the other hole from front to back. Tie a double knot and repeat, bringing the needle through to the front of the circle, through the bead, and out to the back again. Tie the thread off in a double knot and trim the ends. Sew seed beads onto the small circles and 6mm rounds onto the large circles.

10. Attach the circles. Glue a Pearlescent Magenta circle in the center of each of the large circles on the earrings and a Halo Pink Gold circle in the center of each of the medium circles.

MATERIALS

- Black deertan kidskin
- Metallic paint for leather in Metallic Silver, Pearlescent Turquoise, and Pearlescent Blue
- Five 4mm black glass bicones
- Ten 8mm glass bicones (any color, as these will not be visible)
- Ten 12 x 9mm silver textured bead cones
- 15" (38cm) elastic beading cord
- Leather adhesive
- Craft cement adhesive or nail polish (I used G-S Hypo Cement)

TOOLS

- Scissors
- Ruler
- Permanent marker
- Die cutting machine
- Die for 1" (2.5cm) circles
- 1" (2.5cm) flat paintbrush

Winged Orbs Bracelet

Internal diameter: 2⅜" (6cm)

1. Die cut the circles. Cut two pieces of leather measuring approximately 5½" x 6" (14 x 15cm) to fit the die. Place one piece of leather, grain side down, over the die, and then sandwich everything between the two cutting pads. Place the cutting pads with leather and die on the bed of the die cutting machine with the leather facing up. Crank the handle to move the die through the roller (be sure to follow the manufacturer's instructions for your particular machine). Repeat with the second piece of leather and remove all the die-cut 1" (2.5cm) circles from the leather.

2. Paint the circles. Paint a light coat of metallic paint for leather on the grain side of the circles. Paint ten Metallic Silver, ten Pearlescent Turquoise, and five Pearlescent Blue. Keep the remaining circles for another project. Once dry, paint each circle with a second light coat of paint. Allow them to dry before continuing.

3. Apply adhesive. To make a winged bead, you will need five circles of each color. To start, take two circles of the same color and spread adhesive thinly and evenly across one half of the back of each circle, making sure it reaches all the way to the edge.

4. Attach the circles. Press the glued halves of the two circles together. One half of each circle should be unglued.

5. Attach the third circle. Apply adhesive to the unglued half of the second circle. Apply adhesive to one half of a third circle of the same color. Press the glued halves of the circles together.

6. Attach the remaining circles. Continue gluing in this manner to attach the remaining two circles of the same color.

7. Complete the winged bead. Apply adhesive to the unglued halves of the first and last circles and press them together to form the bead.

8. Create the remaining winged beads. Repeat Steps 3–7 to create the remaining winged beads. You will have five total: one Pearlescent Blue, two Pearlescent Turquoise, and two Metallic Silver. Allow them to dry before assembling the bracelet.

9. Cut the elastic. Cut a 12" (30.5cm) length of elastic beading cord.

10. Begin stringing the beads. String a silver leather bead, an 8mm bicone, and a bead cone onto the elastic cord.

11. Continue stringing the beads. Then, string on a 4mm bicone, a bead cone, an 8mm bicone, and a turquoise leather bead.

12. Finish stringing the beads. Continue following the stringing pattern, alternating colors of leather beads, until all of the beads are strung. Make sure that you string an 8mm bicone, a bead cone, a 4mm bicone, a bead cone, and an 8mm bicone between each leather bead.

13. Knot the elastic. Tie a half-knot in the elastic, pulling all the beads firmly together and ensuring that the 8mm bicones are sitting down into the hole of each leather bead and are covered by the bead cones. Tie a second half-knot, pulling both the bracelet cord and the cord ends to tighten the knot. Make two more half-knots to secure the bracelet. Add a dot of craft cement if desired for extra security.

Tip

Pre-stretch your elastic by pulling it several times. This will help minimize overstretching of the elastic with wear.

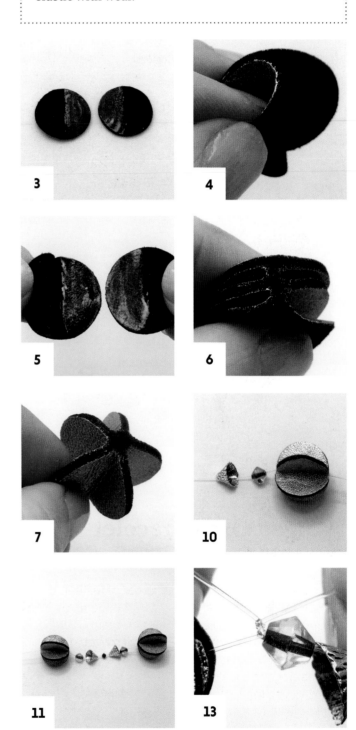

MATERIALS

- Zebra print bracelet blank
- Black bracelet blank
- 10" (25cm)-long rhinestone silver cup chain
- 2 black metal teardrop components
- Two 8 x 10mm silver oval jump rings
- Two 4mm silver jump rings
- 2 silver earring wires
- Multipurpose adhesive (I used 527 Glue)
- Leather adhesive

TOOLS

- Die cutting machine
- Ring die (about 1¼" [3cm] external diameter)
- Scissors
- Ruler
- Permanent marker
- Chain-nose pliers
- Flush cutters
- Toothpick

Zebra Sparkle Earrings

Finished length: 2¼" (5.5cm)

2

3

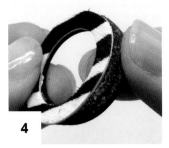

4

5

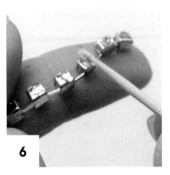

6

7

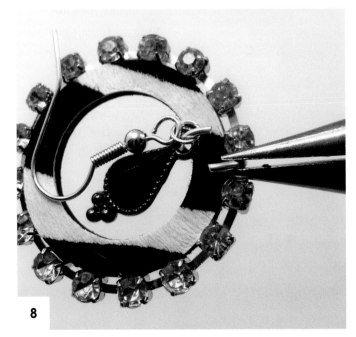

8

1. Prepare the leather. Cut a 3" x 1½" (7.5 x 4cm) strip from the bottom of each bracelet blank. Cut the strips in half so you have two 1½" (4cm) squares of each color.

2. Die cut the rings. Place one square, hair/grain side down, over the top of the ring die. Sandwich the leather and die between the spacer plates and place everything into the bed of the die cutting machine. Place the assembly in the mouth of the machine and turn the handle to feed it through (be sure to follow the manufacturer's instructions for your particular machine). Repeat with all the leather squares. Set the inner circles aside for another project.

3. Apply adhesive. Apply a thin layer of leather adhesive to one black ring and one zebra ring.

4. Glue the rings together. Align the two rings and press them together firmly together. Repeat with the remaining two circles.

5. Cut the chain to length. With the rhinestones facing up, wrap the cup chain around the outside of a pair of glued rings. Cut the chain to the outer circumference of the rings. Repeat with the second set of rings.

6. Apply adhesive. Use the toothpick to apply a dab of multipurpose adhesive to the side walls of the first three or four cups in the chain.

7. Attach the chain. Press the glued cups into place along the edge of one of the ring pairs. Continue applying adhesive to the chain and gluing it to the ring until you have used all the chain. Repeat for the second set of rings.

8. Complete the earrings. Attach a 4mm jump ring to the loop of an earring wire. Open the oval jump ring and hook on the teardrop component. Carefully use the oval jump ring to connect the leather ring and the earring wire. Repeat for the second earring.

Sources and Acknowledgments

A big thank-you to Silver Creek Leather, whose wonderful leather products are featured throughout this book. It is a pleasure to work with leathers that make these designs work so well. I encourage you to visit their website and join them on Facebook for further leather jewelry inspiration. Visit *www.silvercreekleather.com* to learn more.

Most of the materials used in this book are readily available from your local craft store. I used products from the following companies when making the projects for this book. Please feel free to select the materials and products you like and that work best for you as you create your own leather jewelry projects.

Bead Gallery, Bead Treasures, Beadalon (*www.beadalon.com*), Beads 'n Crystals (*www.beadsncrystals.com.au*, filigree components), The BeadSmith (*www.beadsmith.com*, Round Kumihimo Disk, jewelry tubing), Blue Moon Beads (*www.bluemoonbeads.com*), Cousin, Feeling Inspired (*www.feelinginspired.com.au*, beads, chain, and findings), Hoffman Originals (*www.beadsoupandmore.com*, Bead Gravy seed beads), Horizon Group USA, Jacquard (*www.jacquardproducts.com*, Lumiere paint), Jesse James Beads (*www.jessejamesbeads.com*), Sizzix (die cutting machine, dies), Swarovski.

About the Author

Myléne Hillam (pronounced Millane) designs and creates jewelry in her studio in Brisbane, Australia. Her unique and creative designs have resulted in several significant awards, including the prized Craft and Hobby Association (CHA) Designer Press Kit Award. Her work is regularly featured in international craft publications, and she teaches and demonstrates both locally and abroad. With more than twenty years of craft experience, Myléne is passionate about passing her knowledge on to her students in her workshops.

Index

Note: Page numbers in italics indicate projects·

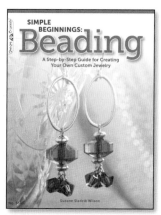

Simple Beginnings: Beading
ISBN 978-1-57421-415-4 **$14.99**
DO5386

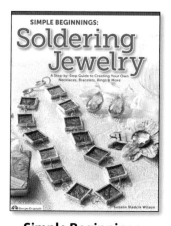

**Simple Beginnings:
Soldering Jewelry**
ISBN 978-1-57421-416-1 **$14.99**
DO5387

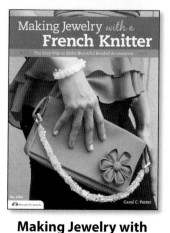

**Making Jewelry with
a French Knitter**
ISBN 978-1-57421-363-8 **$8.99**
DO3486

Bead Weaving on a Loom
ISBN 978-1-57421-384-3 **$8.99**
DO3507

Sewing Leather Accessories
ISBN 978-1-57421-623-3 **$14.99**
DO5313

**Handmade Leather
Bags & Accessories**
ISBN 978-1-57421-716-2 **$19.99**
DO5036

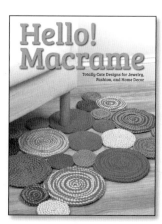

Hello! Macramé
ISBN 978-1-57421-868-8 **$12.99**
DO5442

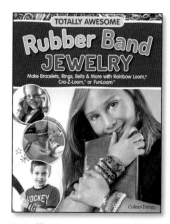

**Totally Awesome Rubber
Band Jewelry**
ISBN 978-1-57421-896-1 **$7.99**
DO5454

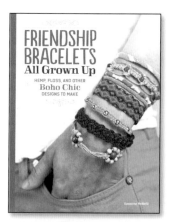

Friendship Bracelets
ISBN 978-1-57421-866-4 **$12.99**
DO5440